THE COPPER KINGS OF MONTANA

THE Copper Kings OF MONTANA

Marian T. Place

ILLUSTRATED BY

ERNEST KURT BARTH

Random House
NEW YORK

Published in New York by Random House, Inc., and simultaneously in Toronto, Canada, by Random House of Canada, Limited.

Library of Congress Catalog Card Number: 61-7779

Manufactured in the United States of America

ESPECIALLY FOR

Sibyl and Bonnie Holbrook

Contents

THE COPPER KINGS OF MONTANA

1

Enter Marcus Daly

In August 1876 a stagecoach sped across a mountain-rimmed, mile-high valley in southwestern Montana. Snow powdered the sheer granite ridge of the Continental Divide on the east. Southward the Highlands glittered in the brilliant sunshine. A volcanic cone rose solitarily on the west. Passage to the north was blocked by a steep hill.

One weary passenger complained, "How much farther is that mining camp anyway?"

A stocky black-haired Irishman named Daly pointed toward the hill. "There it is!"

The impatient man squinted through the swirling dust. "Where?"

"Midway up that barren slope. Can't you see the mine dumps?"

"Is that Butte?"

"It must be Butte," Daly answered.

"I thought the camp would be strung out along the creek," complained the weary passenger. "It's a long haul up that hill."

"So it is," Marcus Daly agreed, but said no more. He was very Irish in speech and appearance, with a bristling black mustache and friendly blue eyes. His face was weathered. His suit coat bulged over powerful arm muscles. He looked what he was—one of the best mine superintendents in the West.

Daly was as anxious to reach Butte as the other passengers. Butte was booming, thanks to recent discoveries of high-grade silver deposits. Every man who had staked a claim along the black-stained ledges outcropping on the hill was positive he had a fortune in sight.

Every newcomer hoped to strike it rich, and Marcus Daly was no exception.

Before long the stagecoach rolled across a bridge spanning Silver Bow Creek. Daly glanced briefly at the abandoned gold placers lining its banks. He was not interested in these worked-out surface diggings. When the horses pounded up the southwest slope, he looked for evidence of underground mining. Moments later he saw an unpainted shaft house. The tall gaunt structure towered over dumps and an ore-crushing mill.

The coach flashed by other workings. Midway up the rocky slope the driver began pulling back on the reins. Ore wagons, canvas-sheeted freighters, wood carts and saddle horses slowed passage along the camp's steep, rutted thoroughfare. Main Street was bordered by a few stores, frame buildings with two-story false fronts, cabins, a stable, a smithy and more mine workings.

"Butte!" the driver bawled as the coach halted in front of the Hotel de Mineral. The small hostelry, Butte's first hotel, was squeezed in between a saloon and the post office, on the southwest corner of Main and Broadway.

Daly alighted first, and slapped the dust from his hat and suit. The moment his valise was tossed onto the planked walk, he picked it up and entered the hotel. A hot soak in a tin tub eased the fatigue of the almost five-hundred-mile journey north from Salt Lake City, Utah. Later a meal of elk steak, beans and strong tea relieved his hunger. However, neither the hot bath nor the food lessened his in-

GROCERY

ner restlessness. He felt like a race horse champing to start a big race.

The goal?

A fortune—millions, and more millions!

Daly had come a long way from the poverty of growing to manhood in County Cavan, Ireland. After emigrating to the United States in 1856, he had worked as a dock laborer and at other odd jobs in New York City.

A few years later he set out for Grass Valley, California. There he obtained work as a mucker, shoveling rough-bottom in a gold mine. Soon he mastered single-jack drilling and learned how to handle explosives. He discovered he liked working underground. He liked mining. So he became a full-fledged miner, earning two dollars for every ten-hour shift underground.

Daly soon realized he would never get rich on these wages, so in 1861 he joined the stampede to the Nevada silver strike. Beginning as a miner in the famous *Comstock* mine, he advanced speedily to shift boss, and foreman. During these years he studied the character of ore bodies. He developed an instinct for finding ore—"a nose for ore." He made himself an expert on underground mining methods. Finally he attained a top position as superintendent of mines.

But he was still not satisfied.

Daly dreamed of being as rich as two former employers: John W. Mackay, the Bonanza King, for whom he had worked as foreman in the *Comstock;* and "Lucky" George Hearst, for whom he had located the *Ontario,* one of the greatest silver producers in all mining history, at Lake Flat, Utah.

After that Daly had put the Midas touch to the *Emma* and *Ophir,* Utah mines owned by the Walker brothers of Salt Lake City. They claimed, "Daly can see farther into the ground than any other man." No wonder they sent him to Butte to examine and possibly purchase the *Alice,* a silver prospect.

Daly sighed, and lighted a cigar. It was a fifty-cent Havana, a rich man's smoke, the kind Mackay and Hearst offered their friends. But the cigar only increased his fidgetiness. He wasn't fooling himself. He was no cigar-smoking gentleman. He never thought of himself as other than a tobacco-chewing miner. He was thirty-four, he reminded himself, and still dragging his boots on his first million. Time was running out on him.

"I've got to make me big strike in Butte!"

Butte was his last chance. The West had already

been fine-combed for new bonanzas. The big gold producers of the fifties and sixties were gradually running out. The fabulous *Comstock* had paid its last big dividend.

Practically all mining these days was underground. Quartz mining, it was called. Locating a good prospect was only the beginning. The gold- or silver-bearing ore had to be extracted from the worthless country rock. Then it was necessary to crush the ore, remove the waste and impurities, and refine the metal before the owner realized one cent of profit.

Sinking a shaft, timbering against cave-ins, blasting, labor and supplies—all these came under the heading of development. Thousands of dollars must be invested in development. Sometimes this investment paid off handsomely. More often it bankrupted a man, or his company of partners. Small wonder that quartz mining had almost brought an end to the day of the one-man mine owner, unless that man was already comfortably rich.

And Daly was not rich. But he could be, he was sure . . . someday. The Walkers had offered him a small interest in the *Alice* if he decided it was worth developing. Even a small share in a good producer could do wonders to a man's pocketbook. The *Alice* might start him on his way!

2

The Alice

Daly tamped out his cigar and strode outside. He walked along narrow twisting streets and by-paths. In every direction mining location notices fluttered from posts. Shaft houses and gallus frames were silhouetted against the intensely blue sky. The air had the invigorating zing of mile-high country.

East of the hotel he came to Town Gulch, a steep gully. Here was the town pump, its rusty neck collared with boards that covered a once-bubbling spring. No flower, no grass sprouted from the decomposed granite soil. A road meandered to the top, or head, of the gulch. Crowded on each side, one stacked almost atop the other, were cabins and shanties and piles of wood, ash, garbage and bottles. These reminded Daly of a poverty-stricken Irish village. Unaware that his future fortune lay underneath this ugly gulch, he turned away quickly.

A short distance above the hotel, up Main Street, Daly strolled into the yard of the *Original* mine. On August 10, 1864, the locators had named it thus because it was the first quartz lode discovered in the district where men had previously panned for raw gold nuggets in stream beds.

"No use rustling here," a workman called out, meaning there was no job available.

"I'm new, and wantin' a bit of news about the camp," Daly answered.

The workman called his helper from sawing mine timbers. Daly offered each a chew of tobacco. They accepted, recognizing him as one of their own kind, in spite of his starched collar and good suit.

They told him that Butte had boomed briefly as a gold placer camp back in 1864. However, the diggings on Silver Bow Creek and others in the near gulches were shallow. The gold was hard to pan, and poor grade. One by one the stampeders pulled stakes until less than fifty remained.

These hangers-on continued scratching away. They named the camp Butte City after Big Butte, the volcanic cone overshadowing the hill.

"There always was silver aplenty in sight," the first workman declared.

"But it was low-grade too—like the gold. Nothin' to skyhoot a man's hopes," his partner added. "Trouble was, the nearest smelter was three thousand miles away. A poor man couldn't afford to ship out his ore by ox team, let alone pay refining charges."

Daly understood. How discouraging to have tons of silver ore and no way to market them profitably. No wonder that by 1875 Butte was almost totally deserted, a ghost town.

"It would have stayed that way if those highfalutin experts had their say," the first workman explained. "They come in here and poked around and told us Butte ores was next to worthless! They said the camp had no future."

"But Bill Farlin showed 'em! He struck high-grade silver in the *Travonia,*" the helper gloated. "Comin' in on the coach, you passed it at the bottom of the southwest slope."

"I remember it," Daly said. "So Farlin sparked new life into Butte, eh?"

"I'll say. Overnight we had a stampede. Everybody scrambled like mad to locate claims, and the temperature was twenty below zero."

Although the stampede was not a big one, Daly learned that over one hundred claims had been recorded. Many were on ground abandoned by those who had not hung on quite long enough.

Soon one and then other ore-concentrating mills were built. Mine owners realized a good profit shipping concentrate largely free of dead-weight waste. All were so encouraged that they hastened to double their output, then triple it.

"If it weren't for development costs, Butte would be blowin' sky-high by now," the workman claimed. "A few mines like the *Travonia,* and the *Great Republic,* and the *Late Acquisition* are makin' some money. But the high cost of quartz mining is forcing more than one good locator to sell out." He eyed Daly. "You interested?"

"I'm interested," Daly answered. He wanted the word to spread. By morning a whole crew of prospectors, anxious to sell their claims, would be knocking on his hotel room door. He felt it wise to see other properties before settling on the *Alice.*

During the following week Marcus Daly inspected numerous prospects. His observations led him to guess (rightly) that the Butte ores occurred in a complex system of fissure vein deposits. The Butte hill was a treasure trove.

But the key to the treasure was development. And that cost a staggering amount of money.

Finally Daly headed for the *Alice*. Hiring a saddle horse, he rode two miles to the top of the hill. Here, on January 2, 1875, Rolla Butcher had discovered an outcropping of silver. He had staked a claim 1,183 feet long and 550 feet wide, and posted his location notices. Then he secured his ownership by recording it. A recorder kept track of the location, size and ownership of all claims in the mining district. Supposedly Butcher named his prospect for a sweetheart.

The *Alice* overlooked the entire slope, the valley below and the shouldering mountains. From it Daly looked down on Big Butte.

"Morning!" Butcher greeted Daly at the collar of the shaft. "Ready to go underground? She's a good one, Mister Daly," he hastened to assure his prospective buyer. "She's showin' fifty thousand, but I'll sell for half that. I ain't got the backing to develop her proper."

Daly stepped onto a crude wood cage suspended over the shaft by a long rope. This rope fed through a pulley on the headframe above, and wound onto a large drum set on the ground near by. A mule was hitched to a horizontal wooden arm connected to the drum. When the mule pushed the arm backward, the rope played out and the cage dropped down the solidly timbered

shaft. When the mule moved forward, the rope rewound, returning the cage to the surface. The crude hoisting apparatus was called a *whim.*

Butcher joined Daly on the cage. It had no sides, but four upright posts supported a crossbar over their heads. The men took hold of the crossbar with their right hands. Next Butcher jerked twice on a signal line running from the crossbar, up through the pulley and over to the whim. A bell clanged twice, and a man called a *puncher* prodded the mule. It began backing up. The cage slowly disappeared down the eight-by-ten-foot shaft.

From bright sunlight the men dropped down into the dark shaft. The cage slipped smoothly along small wooden guides nailed to the walls. Butcher lighted two candles, shielding the tiny flames with his hands.

Thirty feet underground Butcher jerked the line once. The cage stopped. The men stepped out into a *crosscut.* Water dripped from the low roof and trickled down the walls. At five-foot intervals, Butcher had wedged heavy timbers upright to brace the roof of the crosscut against caving. The floor was ankle-deep in cold, wet slime.

After they'd covered a distance of more than twenty feet, Butcher stopped. "Here's the vein," he said, raising his candle. The crosscut intersected the vein at a right angle. To the left and right, Butcher had excavated a *drift* or passageway along the vein.

Daly moved along the tunnel-like drift, examining the partially exposed vein. When he reached the *face* or working end of the drift, he said, "You've got a nice prospect, but I don't see fifty thousand dollars' worth of high-grade showing here."

"There's sixty tons on the dump." Butcher referred to the ore already mined, hand-sorted from waste, and stock-piled on the surface.

"Not enough." When Daly shook his head, the shadows cast by his hat in the candlelight danced crazily along the grim walls. He was a little disappointed. Perhaps he had hoped for too much.

Butcher added hastily, "I opened another lead fifty feet below here. It ain't timbered, but if you're willing——"

"Let's see it."

The two returned to the cage, signaled, and dropped another fifty feet. The crosscut here was cramped, the air bad. Their footsteps slushed hollowly. Lifting his candle, Daly saw rock fragments, large enough to crush a man, hanging loosely like jagged teeth. The hole would have terrified anyone not used to being underground. Even Daly moved

with caution. A sudden, terrifying fall of rock, and he would be buried alive!

Crouching low, he followed Butcher. They reached the vein. With great care Daly loosened a small segment for examination. High-grade! Much richer than that seen above. This drift bored right into a solid body of ore.

He figured rapidly. From its pinched surface outcropping, the vein had widened to five feet at a depth of thirty feet underground. Now, fifty feet lower, it was even wider and richer, and obviously it plunged deeper.

He needed no further proof.

"Mister Butcher," he began, struggling to keep his voice calm, "I'm thinkin' twenty-five thousand dollars is a fair price for the *Alice*. Shall we be goin' back up now, and sign the papers?"

"Yes, sir! You'll never forget buying this prospect, Mister Daly!"

As they slogged back to the cage, Daly was sure of it. He almost shouted for joy.

Once he started developing the *Alice,* he would have a running jump on his first million!

3

Shaft, Crosscut, Drift and Stope

"We will sink the new shaft here," Marcus Daly ordered. He had marked off an area eight by twelve feet near the discovery shaft. "Start digging, boys."

Daly was exuberant. The Walkers had agreed to full-scale development of the *Alice.*

The "boys" were skilled shaftmen imported from the Nevada mines. All were Irish, all intensely loyal to Daly. Because theirs was the most dangerous and most strenuous work, he paid them six dollars a day for a ten-hour shift. This was two dollars more than other mines paid. Off hours these men were building cabins for their families down the hill from the *Alice.* They named their tiny settlement Walkerville, in honor of the mine owners.

Their shovels bit into the loose *overburden.* When bedrock was exposed, they used hand drills to bore holes. These were loaded with giant powder and blasting caps. The "shooter" lighted the fuses. Then the shaft men scrambled for safety.

W-h-o-o-o-m!

Rock and dust hurtled violently into the air. The sound echoed off the east ridge like cannon shot. After the dust settled, the shaftmen cleaned out the hole. Drill, blast, clean up and timber the sides: they would repeat this for months, deepening the shaft about three feet a day. At first they climbed in and out by ladder, skinning up the rungs away from danger as nimbly as cats. Later they were lowered and raised in a new cage run by a steam-powered hoist.

The gallus frame rose twenty-five feet above the shaft. It supported the big shiv-wheel over which the hoisting cable passed from the cage to the drum.

The ruts on Main Street deepened as a constant parade of wagons hauled supplies to the mine. From neighboring forests, wood contractors delivered cordwood to fire the steam boiler and stout timbers to line the new shaft and support the crosscuts and drifts in both the new and the old workings. They also brought in lumber for a fence, the superintendent's office, a smithy, huge ore bins and a concentrating mill. Saws whined and hammers pounded from dawn to dark.

The camp buzzed with talk of the money Daly was spending.

"The man is a fool!" many declared.

"He is not!" his Irishmen argued loyally. "Daly is the smartest mining man in the West."

Chins wagged faster when Daly hired still more men. He meant to improve the original workings and mine from them. Eventually the new and old workings would join underground.

Going to work on Butcher's original shaft, a crew first enlarged the *station,* the opening off the shaft at the thirty-foot level. Next they dug a shallow drain on one side of the crosscut to draw off the water. It trickled into the *sump*, or bottom, of the shaft. A pipe line and pump were installed to lift this water to the surface, and channel it off into a nearby gully.

Butcher's inadequate bracings were supplanted with timber sets placed every five feet the entire

length of the crosscut and drift. Each set consisted of two upright fir posts, ten inches in diameter, placed against the sides. These posts supported a *cap,* or horizontal roof timber. *Square-set timbering,* as this was called, had been perfected in the deep California and Nevada quartz mines. Without these sets to support the ground and prevent major cave-ins, underground mining was impossible.

When a second steam-powered hoist was installed to operate the cage in the discovery shaft, Daly asked his foreman, "All set to lower the mule?"

The man grinned. "Yes, sir." He shouted the order.

The surface crew dropped their tools and gathered to watch the fun. The foreman sent word down to the miners. They congregated at the station.

The mule, Whitey, no longer needed to operate the crude whim, was led to the collar of the shaft. The cage was waiting.

"Careful now! Whitey's got a kick like a charge of powder!"

Suddenly five men tackled the unsuspecting animal. They roped his front and hind legs and put a sack over his head.

Whitey brayed and bucked.

The miners laughed. "Watch out for them hoofs, now!"

"Listen to Whitey sing! He sounds like a banshee."

Dust flew, men struggled, and the mule fought furiously. Gradually he was forced onto the cage and tied down. Daly jerked the signal line twice, and the cage dropped.

S-w-o-o-o-sh!

Whitey's braying echoed eerily up the shaft. Down below the miners greeted the mule with a cheer. Gingerly they untied the ropes, then tugged and heaved to get him into the stall built for him. When he smelled the fresh hay and dried corn in the feed trough, he quieted down.

A miner sighed. "Poor divvil! He'll nivver see daylight again."

His partner said, "Save your tears. That cussed mule will grow fat as a pig, what with our makin' a pet of him, and feedin' him tasties from our lunch pails. Would ye be pushin' ore cars yourself, man, to spare a mule?"

Whitey was not the first mule to work underground. For decades, hundreds of mules and horses had lived out their lives underground in mines. They hauled small cars of ore from the drifts to the cages. All were prime stock, and given excellent care. In Butte the larger mines hired a veterinarian to look after them. The miners nicknamed them, fed them "tasties," and taught them to "sing."

Daly made countless trips underground, superintending all phases of development. He ordered the drifts on each level enlarged, stoutly timbered and advanced along the veins. He decided when the miners should be starting a *stope*.

A stope is one of a series of horizontal cuts excavated *above* a drift. To stope, the miners have to drive up through the vein, generally a solid and continuous mass of ore.

First, over their heads in the drift, the miners blasted an opening eight feet high, eight feet wide, and fifty feet long. They shoveled the broken ore into cars so it could be hoisted to the surface.

Next, the miners used timbers to replace the once-solid rock ceiling. This planked roof then served as the next floor of the stope. Again the miners blasted, and this time the ore was shoveled into chutes built at the side, and fell down the chutes into the waiting ore cars. Once more timbers replaced the once-solid ceiling and served as the next floor. Stoping would continue until all the ore overhead in that particular vein had been removed. Then the entire opening would be filled with waste to prevent a gigantic cave-in. The same process would be carried on in each new level as the mine deepened, new levels being opened every hundred feet underground.

In time the complicated underground workings would begin to resemble a large office building. The shaft would be like the elevator shaft in a building, except that it would reach down below ground level instead of rising above it. In larger mines, the shaft would be compartmented to accommodate two cages: one for lowering men and

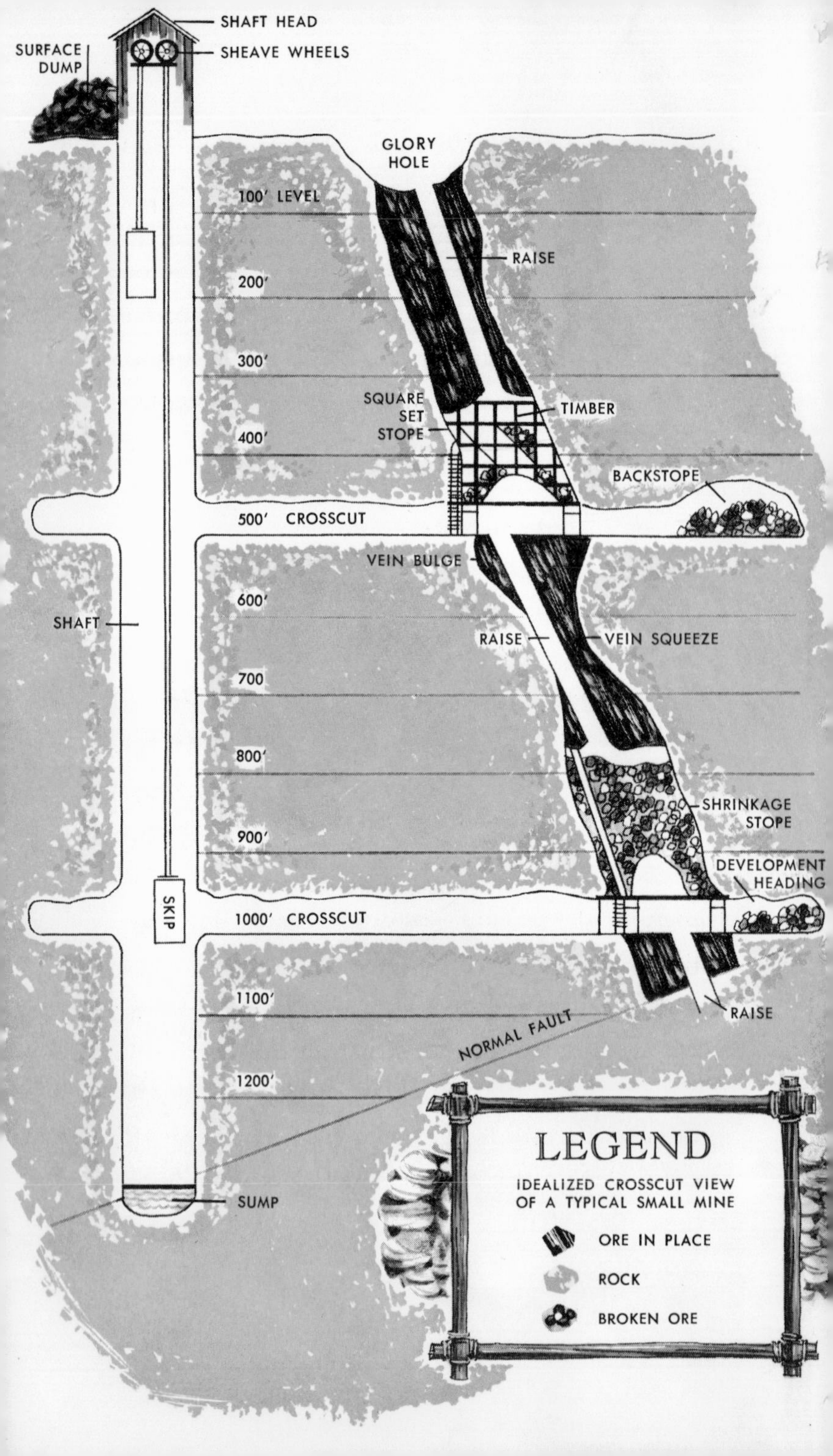
SHAFT HEAD
SHEAVE WHEELS
SURFACE DUMP
GLORY HOLE
100′ LEVEL
RAISE
200′
300′
SQUARE SET STOPE
TIMBER
400′
BACKSTOPE
500′ CROSSCUT
VEIN BULGE
600′
SHAFT
RAISE
VEIN SQUEEZE
700
800′
SHRINKAGE STOPE
900′
DEVELOPMENT HEADING
SKIP
1000′ CROSSCUT
1100′
RAISE
NORMAL FAULT
1200′
SUMP
LEGEND
IDEALIZED CROSSCUT VIEW OF A TYPICAL SMALL MINE
ORE IN PLACE
ROCK
BROKEN ORE

supplies; the other for hoisting ore. Often there was a third compartment to house the pump lines and cables that serviced the mine.

The *levels* would be driven at regular intervals of one hundred feet. They would be similar to the floors in an office building.

The *crosscuts* would be like the corridors on the floors.

The *stopes* would be like the separate offices, except that one would be atop the other with timbered sides, floors and ceilings. Miners used ladders to reach them.

In the *Alice,* and other mines at this time, the

miners worked solely by candlelight. Day shift was from 6:00 A.M. to 4:30 P.M. Night shift was from 6:00 P.M. to 4:30 A.M. Before going underground, miners were given enough candles to provide light during their shift. They called out their names to the shift boss, who put a check mark beside their names in his daybook. No check mark, no pay.

The station at each level underground was dimly lighted. Here the miners picked up small iron spikes that were used as candleholders. Shoving one end of the candle onto the candleholder, they lighted it. Then they walked to wherever they were working. The free end of the candleholder was driven into a crack in the rock, and the men shoveled, timbered and drilled in this flickering, feeble light.

The boxes of blasting powder were stored some distance from the shaft. Some miners stuffed from two to six sticks of powder in their bootlegs and kept them there until needed.

"No more o' that! Are ye wantin' to lose a leg, man?" the shift boss would warn. Few paid attention.

Other miners sometimes warmed the sticks of powder over a burning candle!

"Saints preserve us! Would ye be blowin' us all to smithereens! Once more, Pat, and it's a pink ticket for you." A pink ticket was a discharge slip.

Miners were supposed to wait at a safe distance at least an hour after "shooting a round." Some fuses were slower than others and didn't act properly. Miners returning too soon were often injured or killed by these delayed charges. Daly's men were mostly Irish Catholics. They called these deadly charges "requiem masses" after the church rites for the dead.

If, before going off shift, the shooter knew some sticks had not exploded, he warned the man who would be taking his place on the next shift. "Watch it now, Dennis. There be a couple of requiem masses in the stope."

Falling rock constantly endangered the men. Another hazard was tumbling into chutes. Although it was against mine safety rules, some chanced riding up the shaft on top of a car filled with ore. If the car shifted on the cage, it could catch on the shaft timber and throw the man off the car. He would plunge hundreds of feet to his death.

These early-day miners wore no protective hats or shoes. All day they breathed dust from the drilling and shoveling. Many developed "miner's consumption," or silicosis. No fresh air blew into the workings. The down-draft from the shaft whistled into the levels. But the crosscuts, and especially the stopes, were very hot. Many miners worked stripped to the waist.

After ten hours in the "hot box," they were almost too weary to put on their muck-stained damp clothes, plod back to the station, and ride the cage to the surface. In those days there were no change houses equipped with heat, hot water and lockers where the miners could wash and change into dry, clean clothes. Summer and winter they trudged to their cabins or boarding houses in wet, dirty clothing.

Yet Daly's miners fared better than others. He paid higher wages. He never skimped on timbering. He bought the best equipment and powder. The foreman and shift bosses continually inspected the workings for weakened posts, dangerous rock and fire hazards. The *Alice* even boasted a so-called hospital—a small shack with two cots and first-aid equipment.

Daly was a popular boss. He made a point of calling his men by name. He stopped often to pass a word with them. Sometimes he patted a miner on the back. If the miner's shirt was damp, that meant he had been working hard. If it was dry from slacking on the job, Daly would explode with a few well-chosen cuss words, ending with, "You're fired!"

A slacker never found employment again in a Daly-managed property.

Miners ate their mid-shift meal underground. The shaftmen surfaced and congregated at a spot sheltered from the wind. They brewed strong tea in a bucket and used the tops of their round lunch pails for cups.

Whenever possible, Daly joined his shaftmen. "How's she goin', boys?" he would frequently ask.

From them Daly heard what other mines were doing: who had bought, sold or traded a claim; who was shipping ore, how much and what grade. He filed all this information in his mind.

"You're the talk of the camp, Marcus," one of them spoke out.

Daly chuckled. "Still accusin' me of pouring money down a rat hole?"

"Some are. Most talk is about the wages you pay: six for shaftmen and three-fifty for miners."

Daly smiled. "I never liked working for two dollars a day. And I say, good wages make a good town. That's what we want for Butte."

"Aw, it's more than that, Marcus," another remarked. "It's . . . well, you're not too hoity-toity to swap a chaw with your men."

4

A Letter Sparks a Feud

Before Daly left Salt Lake City, the Walker brothers had instructed him to "establish good business relations" with William Andrews Clark, a wealthy banker and mine owner in Butte. So far Daly hadn't had much time for paying social calls. But one afternoon after he'd been in Butte awhile, Daly decided it was time he paid his respects. He trimmed his mustache, put on his good suit, and rode down the hill to call on Butte's most prominent citizen.

William Andrews Clark greeted his visitor cordi-

ally. “Welcome to Butte, Mr. Daly. I’ve been hearing a great deal about you. Sit down.”

Hat in hand, Daly sat on a straight-backed office chair. He and Clark exchanged the usual small talk about the weather. Meanwhile each studied the other.

Daly was surprised to find Clark a small, light-voiced Irishman. His piercing blue eyes and bushy whiskers reminded him of a wire-haired terrier.

Daly was a little in awe of Clark. He had heard

that, although only thirty-nine, the man already had accumulated a fortune of several million dollars. A former school teacher, Clark had stampeded to the Colorado and Montana gold strikes. He made big profits freighting supplies and selling them, and had also done well in banking. Men said of him, "Clark never put out a dollar that didn't come back with two stuck to it."

In 1872 Clark had bought four Butte prospects for very little money: the *Original, Colusa, Mountain Chief* and *Gambetta.* The following winter he studied geology and mining at the Columbia School of Mines in New York City. But he was too cautious to spend one dollar more than necessary to develop his prospects.

Clark was well educated. Daly was not.

Clark was fastidious and well-groomed. Daly didn't care if his shoes had mine muck on them.

Clark was finicky in speech and manners. He was already becoming something of a snob. Marcus Daly had none of these qualities, and never would.

"Tell me about the *Alice,*" Clark urged his caller.

Daly loved to talk, particularly about his mining activities. He launched into glowing detail about his plans. He was going to make the *Alice* the biggest silver mine in Montana. He was not boasting.

He believed this possible. He disagreed with his friend Mark Twain, who had been a reporter on the Virginia City (Nevada) *Enterprise* when Daly was foreman of the *Comstock.* Twain had quipped, "A mine is a hole in the ground owned by a liar."

Clark was aghast at Daly's program. It would cost several hundred thousand dollars before it returned a cent of profit. As a man more experienced in money matters, he cautioned his young visitor. Did Daly think it wise to gamble so great a sum on a mere expectation?

It was no hunch, Daly stated emphatically. He was positive there were even richer bodies of ore yet to be found in the mine. His "nose for ore" told him so.

Privately Clark decided that if the *Alice* came even halfway to Daly's wild forecast, it would be pure luck. He didn't think much of the way Daly fancied himself as a keen judge of ore deposits. The way Daly spent money alarmed the cautious Clark. Worse, the man was rather uncouth, and spoke with an Irish brogue as thick as flannel.

Outwardly, however, Clark smiled. He gave every indication of wanting to be friends with the *Alice's* superintendent.

The two parted on the best of terms.

After their chat Clark remained absorbed in thought for some time. Daly could be useful to him. Recently Clark had staked a claim almost adjoining the *Alice.* He had recorded it as the *Moulton.* Now he saw where he could save money. He would hold back developing it until Daly proved whether or not there were extensive deposits in the *Alice.* If there were, undoubtedly they extended into the *Moulton.* Both were on the same *lode,* or somewhat continuous metal-bearing vein.

If the *Alice* ore ran out, Daly would have squandered a small fortune. Clark could sell the *Moulton* and lose nothing.

However, if the *Alice* did prove to be a big producer, Clark figured that he might be able to persuade Daly or the owners to *concentrate* the ore at Clark's new mill. The mill had been a real boon to Butte. Many locators were encouraged to develop their prospects into producing mines after Clark opened it. He built the mill primarily to treat the ore from his *Original* mine. But he made handsome profits processing ores for many small operators.

Yes, indeed! He could make a tidy profit if Daly patronized his mill.

Still . . . Clark tapped a finger on his thin lips. He had done business with the Walker brothers.

He hoped to do more. Did they realize how extravagantly this superintendent of theirs was spending their money? Perhaps a friendly hint . . .

Clark wrote the Walker brothers that in his opinion it was wise to "proceed with caution" in investing in Butte. Some mining experts still maintained the ore bodies were shallow, and therefore the future of the camp was limited. Then Clark added that he considered Daly a good man, although obviously a rough bumpkin whose expenditures in the *Alice* were both wasteful and ill-advised.

The Walkers were not the least disturbed by this unasked-for criticism of their superintendent, but they agreed that Daly ought to see the letter.

Naturally Daly was far from pleased when he read Clark's letter calling him a rough bumpkin. He was already very conscious of his lack of education. But when had he had the time or money to acquire the airs and graces of a gentleman? He had won his promotions with brains and brawn. He had spent his money making life pleasant for his wife and two baby daughters. He had helped his parents. He had sent his brothers and sisters money enough to emigrate to America. The little time he had for books had gone into studying to become a United States citizen.

What really rankled was Clark's implying that Daly did not know his business. Some of the greatest financiers in the West considered him a mining expert second to none. They had entrusted him with vast expenditures of their money. Never had he failed to increase their wealth.

Daly's mustache bristled. He would show the little man what Marcus Daly could do!

And he did.

In the next four years Marcus Daly sparked Butte to first place in the nation as a silver-producing camp. Others took courage from Daly's actions. They drove their shafts deeper. They opened one rich silver deposit after another. A rash of headframes broke out all over the hill.

The permanency guaranteed by this quartz mining brought many new families to Butte. Walkerville swelled to fifty dwellings. Clark hired only Cornishmen, small, wiry, superb miners, very clannish. They shunned the Irish and started their own community of Centerville, a mile downhill from Walkerville. The Butte business district expanded to six square blocks. When Charles Meader opened claims on the extreme eastern slope, another "sub-urb" named Meaderville sprouted on the flat below.

Daly kept his shaftmen deepening the *Alice.* Through a crosscut driven at the two-hundred-foot level, his miners opened a new rich vein eight feet wide. On the five hundred they encountered two additional streaks of rich ore.

None of this went to Clark's mill. Daly installed a larger one of twenty iron stamps, each weighing one thousand pounds. The thunder of those stamps crushing the ore seldom ceased. Six other mills rose along the creek, or out on the flat.

With the *Alice* undeniably a great producer and enriching its owners, Clark finally opened up the *Moulton.* But he waited until the *Alice* workings were deep enough so that the water underground in the *Moulton* would drain into the *Alice,* and be pumped out at Daly's expense.

In 1876, when Daly arrived, Butte's population might have numbered 400. By 1880 it had risen to 3,000. There were schools, churches, even an opera house. The Butte Workingmen's Union was organized June 13, 1878, with 261 charter members. Marcus Daly encouraged this union because he felt it would benefit both miners and mine owners.

The next spring Silver Bow County, Montana Territory, was formed, and Butte was designated the county seat. On December 21, 1881, the entire town turned out to cheer the arrival of the first train, the Utah & Northern.

Thanks to Marcus Daly's "nose for ore," his faith in the *Alice* and his demonstrated ability as a developer of a mining property, Butte boomed.

Daly furnished the key to the treasure box and pried the lid wide open.

5

The Richest Hill on Earth

"Mr. Daly! Wait up," a red-faced Irish miner called out.

Marcus Daly stopped on the boardwalk on North Main Street. "Hello, Mike Hickey. What could I be doing for you this fine spring day?"

"I hear you're looking for a new location," Hickey said bluntly.

Daly smiled. "Ever know a miner who wasn't?"

It was 1882. After five years of grueling work in the *Alice,* Daly was not yet a millionaire. In fact, he was nowhere near that goal. Some months earlier the *Alice* ore had begun decreasing in value. That meant decreasing profits for the Walkers and himself. He had advised the owners to sell while they could command a stiff price. They rejected his advice. Daly then sold them his interest in the mine, resigned as superintendent, and looked for another property.

Hickey fished a sample of high-grade from his pocket and handed it to Daly. "How about takin' a look at more like this in the *Anaconda?*"

The sample was so rich that Daly asked, "What's the trouble, Mike?"

No trouble, Hickey stated positively. He and his brother had overextended themselves. They had twenty-five claims, but could not afford the annual assessment work on each. Mining law required that a minimum of one hundred dollars' worth of development be done annually on each claim. Otherwise, ownership was forfeited, and the property could be "jumped" legally by another claimant.

Rather than lose their claims, Mike and Ed Hickey decided to sell all but three. Ed hoped to keep the *St. Lawrence* and *Never Sweat.* Mike wanted a partner with money enough to develop his *Anaconda.*

"I'm down forty-five feet in the *Anaconda,*" Mike went on, rolling the name richly off his tongue.

"I've got high-grade. But to make big money, I've got to sink that shaft deeper. I'm short on cash. If you put up the money to sink the shaft, I'll sell you a one-third interest."

The fact that Hickey did not want to unload the *Anaconda* told Daly the mine was well worth investigating.

The two rode in Daly's open buggy east on Broadway, then angled up Town Gulch Road almost to the crest of the hill. Here they turned right, passed through a gate, and stopped alongside a horse-powered whim.

The south and east boundaries of the *Anaconda* fell away sharply. The view was as breath-taking as that from the *Alice,* which lay two miles northwest and at a higher elevation.

"How long have you had the *Anaconda,* Mike?"

"Staked the claim along this outcrop you see runnin' across here, on October 18, 1875."

"An-a-con-da," Daly said, stressing the third syllable as the word rolled off his tongue. It was that kind of word. "Where ever did you get that name?"

Hickey chuckled. Everyone asked that. While serving in the Union Army during the Civil War, he had read an editorial written by Horace Greeley in the New York *Tribune.* Greeley had predicted, "Grant will encircle Lee's forces and crush them like a giant anaconda." At the time Hickey said he guessed that an anaconda must be some kind of python whose giant coils encircled, then crushed the enemy.

"You know how it is," Hickey added self-consciously. "A prospector finds an outcropping and files a claim. He hopes he's hit a bonanza and will someday end up owning everything in sight." He confessed that that was what he had in mind when the word "anaconda" popped into his mind. He still thought he could be king of the hill if he had money enough to develop the mine.

Daly's blue eyes twinkled. Hickey was bragging like a true son of Erin who had kissed the Blarney stone.

But, after one trip underground, Daly gladly paid Hickey $15,000 for a one-third share in the *Anaconda.* Sinking the shaft an additional forty feet gobbled up this money. Despite the fact that the shaft opened up a larger vein, Hickey decided to sell out. He felt, rightly, that the mine called for expenditures far beyond his means. "Give me another $70,000, and she's all yours," he offered Daly.

Even if Daly could have scraped together the purchase price, he would have had nothing left for development. The only answer lay in a partnership. He took an option to buy the mine. Then, in a carefully detailed letter, he offered the Walker brothers a three-quarters interest for the $70,000.

They turned him down.

Undismayed, Daly took the train to San Francisco and contacted his old friend George Hearst.

Hearst and Daly had several things in common. Both were born to poverty, were self-educated, and had learned mining the hard way. Both had a nose for ore and the Midas touch. Thanks to Daly's urging him to buy the *Ontario* years earlier, Hearst was now wealthy. He also towered over Daly physically, being six feet tall, with a blanket-sized beard and a large nose.

Hearst's second stroke of good fortune came in locating the *Homestake* in Deadwood Gulch, Dakota Territory. There, for $70,000, Hearst bought an unproved gold prospect that ultimately would prove the world's richest gold mine and pay $160,000,000 in dividends.

Hearst was very interested when Daly stated that the *Anaconda* would equal the *Ontario* as a silver producer. Development would run well over a million dollars, but the eventual profits would be many times that.

At this time Hearst's ready cash was tied up in

developing the *Homestake.* Since he trusted Daly's judgment implicitly, he said, "Let me talk to my partners."

Hearst's partners were two of the wealthiest, most influential men in the West: James Ben Ali Haggin and Lloyd Tevis.

Haggin, son of a Kentucky lawyer and Christian Turkish mother, was a lawyer with investments in mining, railroad, telegraph and express companies. His long-time friend and law partner, another Kentuckian named Tevis, was president of Wells, Fargo & Company, the great Western stagecoach and shipping firm. Both men were partners with Hearst in the *Ontario* and *Homestake.*

Hearst, Haggin and Tevis agreed to purchase the *Anaconda,* giving Daly free a one-fourth interest. They formed the Anaconda Silver Mining Com-

pany and named Daly the general manager.

Haggin signed a book of blank checks and tossed it across the desk to Daly. "In mining you have to spend money to make money. Let me know when you need more. On your way, Mark."

On-your-way, on-your-way, on-your-way . . . The words clicked through Daly's brain as the railroad bore him back to Butte. He could hardly wait to tell his wife that at last he was really on his way to great wealth.

The next day he began issuing orders that raised the dust above and below ground. He hired Michael Carroll to superintend the actual mining, and many of the Irish shaftmen and miners Daly had brought to the *Alice* now switched to the *Anaconda.*

During the summer and fall, the shaft deepened; new crosscuts and drifts advanced along the rich vein. A steam-powered hoist replaced the whim. The shiv-wheel atop the headframe spun forward and back in almost endless motion, raising and lowering the cage. Giant five-ton ore wagons, their axles squealing, lumbered down the gulch road.

"Daly's hit it again," his miners bragged. "He sure has the Midas touch."

Scarcely an issue of the Butte *Miner* appeared without some favorable mention of Marcus Daly. The "very popular general manager" was credited with being a mining genius, an expert on Butte's complex ore bodies, a great benefactor.

These compliments irritated William Andrews Clark. He felt Daly was wasteful, took unreasonable chances, and was no genius—only abominably lucky. He complained to close friends that he, Clark, had opened up more properties, uncovered more ore, mined more scientifically, hired more men, and spent less than half as much money doing so. Clark also stressed the fact that he risked only his own money. He did not gamble with other men's dollars as Daly did.

Clark was disgusted with Daly's habits: The way Daly soiled his trousers sitting on boardwalks and talking to every Tom, Dick and Harry. The way he fraternized with his workmen and swapped tobacco with them. The way he flaunted being Irish and hired only Irishmen whose noisy families had taken over Town Gulch so that now it was called Dublin Gulch.

Yet, for business reasons, Clark continued to maintain a cordial relationship with Daly. After Clark's brother, J. Ross Clark, married Mrs. Daly's sister, there was an added obligation to remain surface-friendly.

Clark fumed. What would the people in Butte say if they knew Marcus Daly had run into serious trouble in the *Anaconda?* Suppose they were to find out that already the big silver producer was running out? Daly's big talk was just so much wind!

Clark had learned that of the last eight thousand tons of *Anaconda* ore concentrated, the output had averaged sixty percent copper, and only forty percent silver. Thus, as a silver producer, the *Anaconda* was a failure!

What would George Hearst and his partners say if they knew that? Really, someone ought to warn them, Clark thought. Wouldn't they be grateful?

It was not hard for Clark to convince himself that he should be the one to enlighten the Syndicate, as the Hearst-Haggin-Tevis partnership was called. So once more he wrote a letter criticizing Daly for being wasteful, ill-advised and "not a gentleman."

But the Syndicate already knew of Daly's problem. He had reported in full, but he had also hinted at something so extraordinary, so secret, that he would not risk writing the details. After reading Daly's report, Hearst took the train to Butte. Daly quickly explained the situation to the great mining magnate.

Because of the hours spent talking with miners from all over the camp, Daly knew more than any one else about underground Butte. He had learned that practically all the veins ran heavily to high-grade silver from the surface down as far as four hundred feet below. But the deeper the mining, the more the silver thinned out and ran to copper.

"Copper!" Hearst exclaimed.

At this time most mining men still considered copper a nuisance metal, of small use and little value. However, Hearst and Daly were men of uncommon insight. They realized the copper situation was changing. Newspapers in the East were extolling "Mr. Bell's telephone instrument." No longer a curiosity, it was a nineteenth century miracle.

Bell had used copper wire to transmit speech. And now some of New York City's streets were being lighted by electricity, thanks to hard-drawn copper wire and copper cable.

More significant to Hearst's and Daly's interests was the fact that the United States was having to import copper to meet the demand. Mines in northern Michigan were producing some, but not enough.

"You've run into copper in the *Anaconda?*" Hearst asked. "Is that what you were hinting at in your letter?"

"You'll see."

Daly and Superintendent Carroll accompanied Hearst underground. The cage dropped to the three-hundred foot level. The station was deserted. Lighting candles, the three moved along a crosscut.

"Look at this!"

Hearst looked, and gasped. *"Chalcocite!"* he exclaimed, recognizing the sooty-colored ore. "A vein five feet wide! But that's impossible. Copper glance has never been found in massive veins like this anywhere in the world."

Daly assured Hearst it was chalcocite, or copper glance. When Superintendent Carroll had brought him the first samples, Daly had recognized them instantly. After inspecting the discovery, he had sworn Carroll to secrecy and stopped all work on the three-hundred. Next he had the samples *assayed,* or analyzed. They showed fifty percent copper, with traces of gold and silver.

"I ran into copper in the *Alice* at the top of the hill," Daly told Hearst. And he went on to explain that he knew Clark was finding copper in the *Original,* midway of the hill and west of the *Anaconda.* Joe Parks had opened a vein in his *Parrott* mine, almost directly below the *Anaconda,* while rumor said Meader was disappointed at finding the sooty ore in his claims on the extreme east slope.

Hearst saw what Daly was getting at. Daly was saying that one of the greatest deposits of copper ever known to man lay in the huge Butte hill!

Hearst already controlled the world's largest gold and silver mines. Now he was fired with the idea of having an interest in possibly the world's largest copper mine.

But was one mine enough, he wondered? Shouldn't Daly buy up surrounding claims?

Daly agreed. Would the Syndicate keep quiet and let him proceed in his own way? He told Hearst how he figured to get control of the two mines located on the same extensive outcropping as the *Anaconda,* without paying an exorbitant price.

Hearst approved, and promised to back Daly to the limit.

Meantime, rumor that the *Anaconda* was a failure had swept through the camp. Hearst's appearance seemed to confirm this. Heads wagged. Gloom settled.

The miners at the *Anaconda* were stunned at being told, "Pull the pumps, boys. We're shutting down."

Immediately other mine owners panicked. They, too, had run into copper, but were unaware of its value. In the following weeks they closed their mines. Shiv-wheels stopped turning. Cages hung idle. Mill stamps ceased dropping.

Clark laid off most of his workers. But he did not offer to sell out, as some did. He could afford to play a waiting game.

"The good days are over," the miners mourned. "Butte is busted!"

Daly seemed to be doing nothing. But he shipped some raw chalcocite to far-off Swansea, Wales, in the British Isles. The world's finest copper smelters were there. He hoped to learn whether or not this ore could be refined and still return a profit. Weeks passed. Finally Daly heard from Wales.

Yes, the chalcocite could be refined successfully.

The smeltermen were amazed at the richness of the Butte ore. By chance, they asked, had it been treated beforehand to remove some of the impurities?

Of course it had not. Daly almost whooped for joy. But he must wait a bit longer.

Very secretly, through men loyal to him but not publicly identified with him, Daly bought up the *St. Lawrence,* adjoining the *Anaconda* on the east. He also purchased the *Never Sweat,* at a slightly lower elevation to the west. The *Never Sweat* was so named because of its cold underground workings.

With the addition of these mines, Daly and the Syndicate now possessed full rights to a massive body of copper ore of untold wealth.

Daly now announced his great discovery to Butte, and the world. Butte was a treasure trove of copper, he said. His company was reopening its *three* mines immediately. They would spend millions developing them. Butte's prosperity was assured for years and years to come.

Proudly Daly concluded by saying, "Butte is the richest hill on earth!"

6

Full Steam Ahead

By 1884 seven tall smokestacks crowned the Butte hill as Marcus Daly poured millions into developing the *Anaconda.* Firemen fed the seven boilers ton after ton of coal to make steam to provide power for the increasing operations.

Morning and night the deep-throated mine whistle tolled hundreds to work. On all sides, a hundred other whistles piped and tooted.

Atop the *Anaconda's* giant headframe, shiv-wheels whined their high thin song. Cages flicked up and down: four decks on a string hoisting ore through one compartment, and triple-decked cages lowering men and supplies in another compartment. In the hoisting room the bells rang constantly, clanging out their different signals.

The traffic in the mine yard was constant. Empty wagons trundled through the gate; loaded ones rumbled out. The noise was deafening: the crash of heavy timbers being stock-piled; of powder boxes being stacked; of ore roaring into bins and out of chutes into wagons; of carpenters, steam-fitters and the blacksmith pounding. During sub-zero weather, the noise sharpened to an excruciating pitch. It mellowed with the spring thaw, when the yard was hock-deep in mud. By summer a pall of dust dulled the golden sunlight and deep blue sky.

Underground the down-draft whistled eerily in the shaft. Cables rattled and cages squeaked as they plummeted and hung open-mouthed at the stations. These were vast lamplighted caverns now, housing mule stalls and auxiliary pumps. The floors were crisscrossed with narrow-gauge tracks leading from the stations into various crosscuts, like the ribs of a fan. Although the traffic in the stations was congested, the racket was muffled by the surrounding rock and dust. Hammers pounded as the square-set timbers advanced; pumps sucked and gurgled; the drifts throbbed with staccato drilling.

or rounds of blasting.

If the underground workings of the *Alice* could be said to resemble the skeleton of an office building, those of the *Anaconda* and adjoining *St. Lawrence* and *Never Sweat* in time approximated a skyscraper.

In 1882 Butte's mines had produced ore valued at almost seven million dollars. This was largely silver production. In 1884, the figure jumped to sixteen million. Butte was still considered a silver camp, and silver continued to dominate the Montana scene until 1887, when copper forged ahead. Years would pass, and millions upon millions would be spent in development, before the Anaconda Company reached the goal envisioned by Daly—that of becoming the world's largest producer of nonferrous metals.

Development costs in all properties drove out the one-man or financially weak partnerships with the exception of Clark, and soon new companies appeared on the scene, all backed by wealthy easterners. The Lewisohn brothers, Leonard and Adolph, of New York bought up Meader's claim on the east slope. They formed the Boston and Montana Consolidated Copper and Silver Mining Company. Their big mine was to be the *Leonard,* but they also developed the *Mountain View, East*

Colusa, Comanche, Moose, Badger State, Greenleaf and other mines.

A French syndicate paid several million for the *Lexington* mine and mill located at Centerville.

Later, influential Bostonians formed the Butte & Boston Consolidated Mining Company. Their properties had such unusual names as the *Free for All, Lone Tree, Blue Jay, Berkeley, Gray Rock, Michael Davitt, La Plata* and the *Sister.*

Although there were other smaller companies, they did not become involved in the budding war of the copper kings to control the entire hill.

Up until now Marcus Daly was a big name and power only in Butte. But the development of the *Anaconda* and its sister mines became only a part of Daly's and the Syndicate's spreading control over the entire Territory. Daly's biggest move outside of Butte was to create a brand-new town.

Since Silver Bow Creek, long since dirtied with mill tailings, furnished barely enough water for the Butte mills, Daly sought another nearby location to build a huge smelter. He found a site only twenty-six miles west of Butte on Warm Springs Creek. Standing on the steep hillside in the shadow of towering Pintlar Peak, Daly decided to build the smelter there. Pointing to a wild hay pasture where elk grazed below, he told his engineers, "We

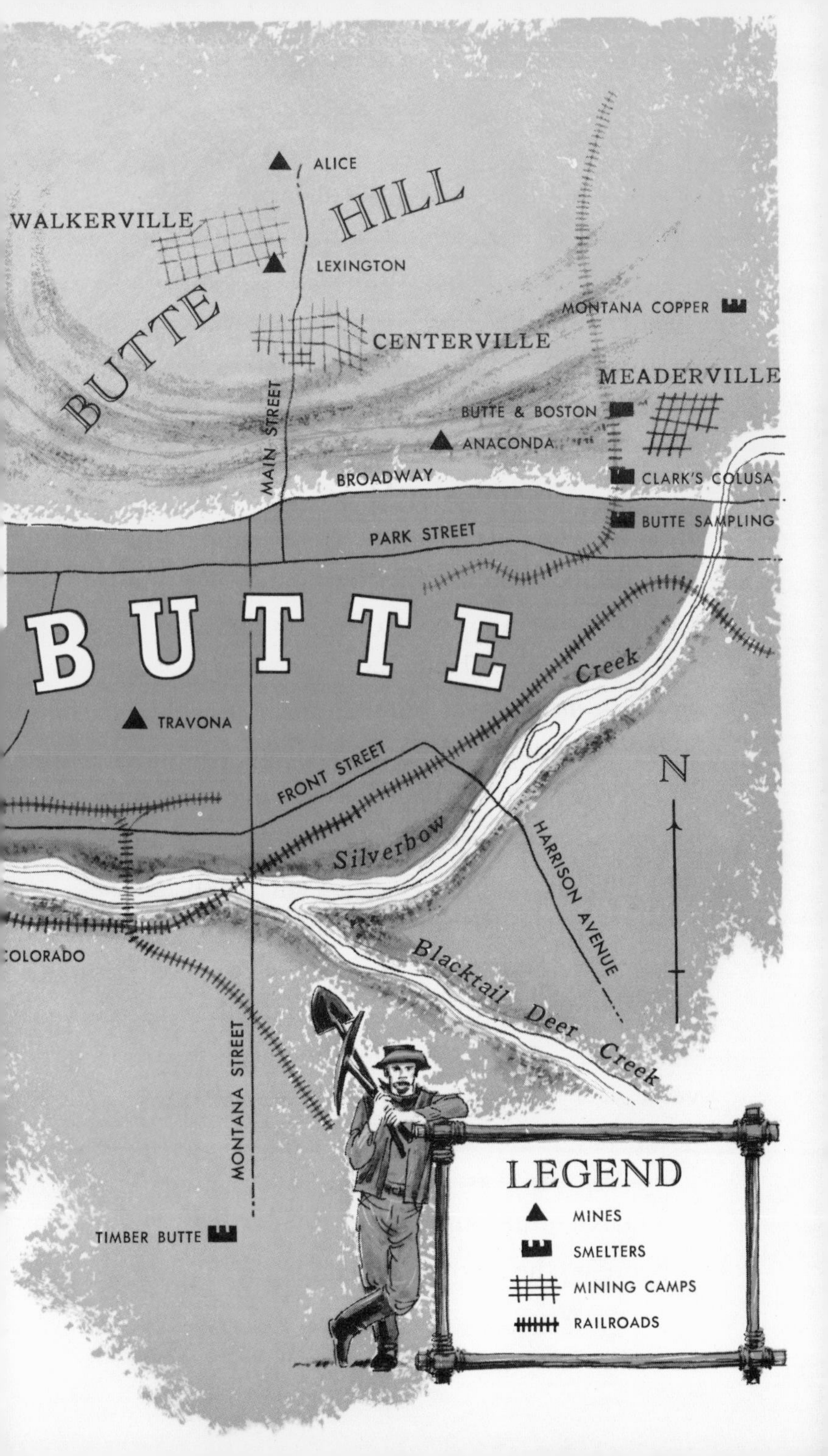
ALICE
WALKERVILLE
HILL
BUTTE
LEXINGTON
MONTANA COPPER
CENTERVILLE
MEADERVILLE
BUTTE & BOSTON
ANACONDA
MAIN STREET
BROADWAY
CLARK'S COLUSA
BUTTE SAMPLING
PARK STREET
BUTTE
Creek
TRAVONA
FRONT STREET
N
Silverbow
HARRISON AVENUE
COLORADO
Blacktail Deer Creek
MONTANA STREET
TIMBER BUTTE
LEGEND
MINES
SMELTERS
MINING CAMPS
RAILROADS

will build a town down there to house the smelter men. We will call it Anaconda."

Mines, a smelter and a new town called for tremendous amounts of timber. Daly talked the Syndicate and the Northern Pacific Railway into investing one million dollars apiece to form the Montana Improvement Company. Through this, Daly obtained control of all timber growing on nine hundred miles of Montana and Idaho railroad right of way. He guaranteed to supply the Northern Pacific's needs for ties and other lumber. In turn he was allowed to ship timber for his mines over the railroad at half the usual freight cost. Soon hundreds of lumberjacks started slashing away at western Montana's virgin stands of prime fir, spruce and pine. Three huge sawmills converted the rough logs into stulls, caps, ten-by-tens and finished lumber.

But the boilers and smelter had to be fueled with coal and coke. To insure a steady supply Daly bought large deposits in neighboring counties.

In all these transactions financed by the Syndicate, Daly always garnered a portion that was solely his.

At last, he was a millionaire.

Then a multimillionaire!

Soon, as he had dreamed, he was recognized as

a mining colossus, a magnate wielding great power over the lives and fortunes of many men, and much of the northern Rocky Mountain region. Yet he remained a friendly, modest man, savoring close kinship with many of his miners. He arranged profitable leases and contracts for the best of his Irishmen. Unlike Hearst, who had little use for scientifically trained men, Daly added to his staff some of the best surveyors, geologists and metallurgists in the United States. The Anaconda smelter rated second to none in the world.

Nor had William Andrews Clark been idle. He now owned forty-six claims and mined silver and copper. He had built small mills and a smelter, founded the Silver Bow Water Works, expanded his bank and also purchased timber and coal lands. After he bought the popular newspaper, the Butte *Miner,* the townspeople read even more about his boasted accomplishments.

Outwardly Clark remained Daly's friend. Privately he grew more and more jealous of Daly's undeniable popularity. Except for his contacts with a few close friends and his family, Clark became more snobbish, more unapproachable. Yet vanity made him seek invitations to make speeches at Territorial conventions and holiday celebrations.

Butte changed too. Once a haphazard camp of

a few clapboard and log cabins, it now sprawled out over the hill and flat with many fine buildings. Most of the Irish crowded into Dublin Gulch and Walkerville. Others spilled over into Meaderville, and tiny settlements known as Chicken Flats, Dogtown, South Butte, Corktown, Hungry Hill, Nanny Goat Hill and Seldom Seen.

The Cornishmen, or "Cousin Jacks," as they were always called, clung to Centerville. In spotless kitchens their wives concocted their pasty. Inside half of a square of rich pastry, they put finely cut tidbits of steak, sliced potatoes, sliced onions, salt and pepper. This filling was covered with the remaining half of dough, and the edges were crimped together. An hour later the pasties were taken from the oven, golden-brown and exuding a heavenly aroma. They were served with "lashings" of brown seasoned gravy.

Thousands of rawboned men poured into Butte to work in the mines. Many were single, and lived in big, drafty boarding houses. They worked hard and played hard, and gave Butte a reputation for around-the-clock brawling. A black eye was considered a badge of honor. These miners fought with their fists, and never wore guns. Butte never needed a city marshal like Wyatt Earp to keep the peace. The policemen, being Irish, understood that

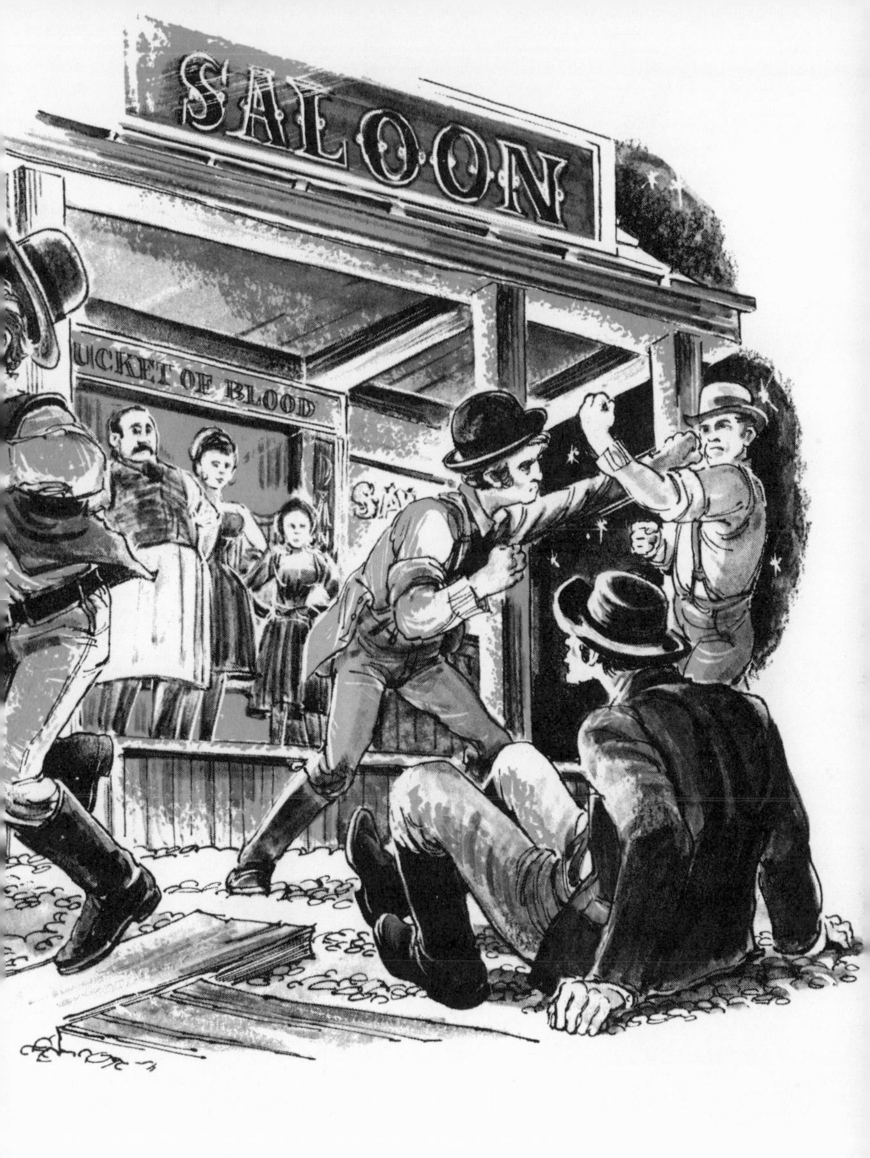

their Irish friends needed to let off steam, and they rarely intervened in these "friendly" fights. The miners' favorite hangouts were called the Big

Stope, the Atlantic, Casino, Arena, Water Hole, Open All Night, Pick and Shovel and the Bucket of Blood.

Butte abounded in saloons, dance halls and theaters. There was a roller-skating rink and, in winter, several ice-skating rinks. Cornishmen loved dog racing, so before long there was also a race track, far out on the flat east of the mountain of copper. Butte men gambled on boxing matches, dog races and cockfights. But their wives siphoned off enough to build churches by staging suppers, carnivals and benefits.

Butte had almost as many horses as people. Each mine boasted long barns and a veterinarian. Livery stables in town outnumbered every other business except the saloons. Horses hauled ore wagons, brewery wagons, lumber wagons, grocers' carts, the fire engine and pump carts, buggies and surreys, hacks and stagecoaches, whims, underground ore trains, the "hurry up" (police) wagon and the hearse.

Most of all, Butte loved parades.

On St. Patrick's Day, Daly gave his miners a holiday. They pinned cloth shamrocks to their coats and hatbands. They gathered in two big groups, one to march down the hill from Walkerville, the other to step along East Broadway from

Dublin Gulch. Supposedly the two were to join at Main and Broadway, and march through the prosperous business district.

Closer and closer the two approached, brass bands clearing the way. The Dublin Gulchers arrived at Main and Broadway first, and swung downhill in the lead. The Walkervilles took offense. They charged the Gulchers. The parade erupted in a free-for-all. Fighting with fists wasn't enough. Soon hitching posts, signs, trash cans and cobblestones were being heaved in every direction.

The merchants, fearing for their windows, hollered, "Help, police!"

But the policemen were also Irish, and emotionally involved in the fray. Finally a group of young men hauled the pump cart from the fire station on Quartz Street, connected the hose to a standpipe and broke up the riot with a stream of icy water. Everyone claimed victory and retired to the closest saloon to quench his thirst by drinking beer that had been colored green in honor of the day.

On June thirteenth, known as Miners Union Day, the mines shut down and all businesses closed. Far up Main Street a brass band assembled. Out in front were horsemen carrying the Stars and Stripes, the Territorial Flag and the Union Banner. Behind this came the Mayor's buggy, usually

with William Andrews Clark sitting next to that worthy Irish official.

Following the band, which made up in gusto for what it lacked in musicianship, came the miners. They marched six abreast, dressed in their best suits and caps, their gold watch chains glittering in the sunlight. Women, children and older people cheered their passing. Afterward, all gathered on the flat for a community picnic, speeches, a drill-

ing contest, sports program and giant fireworks extravaganza.

This was "the greatest mining camp on earth" putting its best foot forward, proud of its rich mines, its thousands of miners, and the untold wealth the vast camp was contributing to the nation's economy.

This was Butte, poised for the opening skirmish in "The War of the Copper Kings."

7

Daly Makes an Enemy

"Have you ever thought of going into politics?"

Will Clark asked this question of Marcus Daly while they were enjoying coffee and cigars in the sumptuous library of the new Clark mansion. It was a three-storied, ornate brick home on one of the best residential streets of the Butte hill.

Daly shook his head. He admitted readily that he was no good at making speeches. His conversation had refined somewhat since his arrival in Butte. He was better groomed now and had less the look of a miner. But he was still very conscious of his educational and cultural limitations. By nature he preferred to mingle with men rather than talk down to them from a platform.

Though radically different in many ways, Clark and Daly had two things in common. Both were Democrats. Both contributed generously to the party election fund.

Clark pointed out that the time had come for the two of them to become more active in politics. Politicians in the Territorial government were taxing mining properties heavily. Too heavily, Clark thought. It was the duty of the mine owners to see to it that henceforth candidates were elected who would vote against increases in mining taxes and other hostile legislation. They had thousands of men working for them. They could control the Democratic vote in Montana. And it was high time they did, Clark asserted.

Daly agreed.

Clark stood before his elaborately carved fireplace mantel. Because he was short, he always stood tall, with bony shoulders thrown back and bushy red whiskers thrust forward. He said, "I have been asked to run as the Democratic candidate for the office of the Montana Territorial delegate to the United States Congress." Of course, he wasn't exactly surprised. He had hinted to friends that he

was "available." And why not? He had business connections throughout Montana. He owned a leading newspaper. He liked to make speeches. He hobnobbed with all the important people, not only in Montana but throughout the nation.

And it just happened that the Democratic party

wanted a wealthy man for a candidate, one vain enough to spend the money necessary to conduct a winning campaign.

Clark had asked Daly if the latter were interested in politics because he had heard that Daly had been asked to run for the office. He was relieved to know that Daly was not interested. But Daly could send a lot of votes his way. Clark mentioned that a word from Daly to his miners on how to vote "would be very helpful."

Daly assured Clark of his support.

Shortly after, through his well-staffed newspaper, the Butte *Miner,* William Andrews Clark announced his candidacy for the impressive Territorial post. The campaign moved ahead smoothly. Clark called at his mines, and from his buggy talked to his foremen. He made speeches in Butte and neighboring cities. The word went out to all Clark's enterprises that the employees should vote for the boss.

Clark seldom visited the Silver Bow Club, a small private group of Butte's wealthiest and most influential men. Others could relax, but not Clark. He spent every waking moment engrossed in making money. But now Clark dropped into the club to play a little poker. He lost consistently, but graciously.

Small wonder that Clark expected to win easily over his Republican opponent, Thomas H. Carter. Carter was young, inexperienced, a former book salesman, a nobody.

The two copper kings saw little of each other during the closing weeks of the campaign. Clark was occupied with running his empire and electioneering, while Daly—unknown to most of the people in the Territory—suddenly found himself facing complete ruin!

When Daly had formed the Montana Improvement Company in 1882 to provide unlimited timber for his mines and smelter, he thought he was fully protecting himself. His mining operations depended on a steady supply of timber. Without such a supply, the Anaconda operations would come to a grinding halt. No timber, no underground mining. Losses in the millions of dollars would be suffered by Daly and the Syndicate, the workers, and the merchants of Butte and Anaconda.

The officers of the Montana Improvement Company included A. B. Hammond and R. A. Eddy. When Daly ordered forty thousand feet of lumber delivered daily to his mines, these men saw to it the order was filled. However, they used dishonest means to do so.

At this time, government-owned lands in the Montana Territory still were not surveyed. Congress had granted the Northern Pacific Railway every other section of land along its right of way. And the Montana Improvement Company had the right to cut timber only on those sections granted the railroad.

Instead, the company poached on other government-owned lands. They stripped them of timber to which they had no right. They did this deliberately over a period of years, at considerable profit.

Complaints were placed before the Secretary of the Interior, Henry M. Teller. A former Coloradan, Teller was sympathetic to mining interests. He ignored the complaints. The timber raids continued unhampered.

Then a man who favored conservation of the nation's natural resources became President of the United States. He was Grover Cleveland. He ordered the Commissioner of Public Lands to investigate the Montana timber raids. In October 1885 the Commissioner stated publicly, "The depredations upon public timber are universal, flagrant and limitless."

Both criminal and civil suits were brought against the Montana Improvement Company and the Northern Pacific Railway. Many months passed while attorneys for both sides gathered evidence.

If the government won the suit and proved the charges of depredations, all timber cutting would cease immediately. It would not resume until all the land in dispute had been surveyed. This project might take several years.

Daly was asked to make a statement about these charges. In the Butte *Miner,* he was quoted as saying, "We understand there is a move to stop cutting timber on public lands. If successful, it will stop all the principal mines in this Territory, and throw out of employment thousands of people. The companies we represent support directly and indirectly ten thousand people, and we know this would be disastrous."

The court hearing of the charges began in Washington, D. C. and dragged on for weeks. Through friends there, A. B. Hammond of the Montana Improvement Company learned secretly that the decision would be delayed until after the November 1888 election. But the decision unquestionably would go *against* Daly's corporation. Not only would Daly be forced to shut down all operations for months; his company would also have to pay several millions of dollars for the unlawfully acquired timber.

Thus Daly faced terrible disaster.

As soon as Hammond received the secret information, he and Eddy rushed to Butte. There they conferred with Daly, telling him of a scheme they had thought up to beat their problems.

The Republicans were going to win this election, they said. It was a foregone conclusion. Benjamin Harrison would be named President of the United States, and the Republican party would control the Senate and House of Representatives.

Now, they pointed out, if William Andrews Clark were elected (and he couldn't lose in a Democrat-controlled Territory), he would go to Washington with two strikes against him: he was a Democrat and he was a mining man. He would be powerless to win the coöperation of fellow congressmen on measures that would assist the mining interests of the West.

Therefore, Hammond contended, salvation lay in electing the Republican candidate, Thomas H. Carter. Hammond implied that he had talked to Carter. In return for their support, Carter supposedly promised to do everything in his power to quash the federal indictments threatening the Montana Improvement Company.

Daly was astonished. Switch sides the week before the election? Elect a Republican! Hammond said that they really had no other choice.

Daly asked for time to think it over.

If Clark won, Daly feared his empire would collapse. He owed it to Hearst, Haggin and Tevis to protect the millions they had poured into the Anaconda Company. Also, he was genuinely fond of Butte, and especially of his town, Anaconda. He didn't want the people to suffer.

On the other hand, if Clark were defeated, the only thing to suffer would be Clark's vanity. And no doubt the thought of Clark's vanity reminded Daly of the letters Clark had written to the Walkers and Hearst. What an opportunity Daly now possessed to give the vain, pompous little man a long-deserved comeuppance! Why not "upset Clark's ore wagon," to use a popular miner's saying.

Of course, upsetting Clark's ore wagon was a minor matter—a strictly personal one. The important thing to Daly was to protect his own company and those dependent on it.

Daly agreed to switch sides and pull the victory right out from under an unsuspecting Clark.

In Butte, Anaconda and the widespread coal and lumber areas enjoying Daly's patronage, word seeped out that whoever wanted to keep his job or business had better vote for Thomas H. Carter.

Cases of whiskey and tobacco arrived unexpectedly at the lumber camps and sawmills. The men were urged to vote for Carter.

Because Daly was so popular, his men and many others were glad to do him a favor.

Apparently neither Clark, in asking Daly to swing votes his way, nor Daly, in influencing men to vote first one way and then the other, felt he was doing anything morally wrong. Equally regrettable, the miners and others cherished so little their right to vote as free men that they surrendered their votes in return for temporary favors. It was the way of the frontier.

Clark used similar tactics. Gallons of his free liquor soothed throats hoarse from cheering for Clark at trumped-up rallies. Clark even shipped special liquor, flares and fireworks into Butte to stage a gigantic victory parade.

But when the time came for a victory parade, Thomas H. Carter was riding out in front. He had won the election.

Clark was stunned—too stunned at first to realize what had happened. Then his campaign lieutenants began asking questions. Slowly the truth emerged. Clark had been betrayed! And by a close friend, an illiterate shanty Irishman! By a shirttail relation, his brother's wife's brother-in-law!

Clark's whiskers bristled. His white face darkened with rage. He wrote a close friend, Martin Maginnis, "The conspiracy was a gigantic one, well planned and well carried out."

In another letter, Clark wrote, "I cannot understand it. There had been no business difficulties between Daly and me, and never an unkind word had been spoken between us. [Evidently Clark had forgotten the unkind letters he had penned in the past.] It was simply an envious and diabolical desire on his part to forever destroy my political influence in the territory."

Eventually this statement was printed in the *Congressional Record.*

When interviewed by a reporter from the St. Paul (Minnesota) *Pioneer Press,* Clark said, "There was a combination against me which could not be beaten." He said that miners at the *Anaconda* were instructed to vote for Carter, and shift bosses were placed at the polling places to see that they did.

To his friends Clark confided that he had always "mistrusted" Daly. He seemed to have forgotten his previous attempts to discredit Daly, and the fact that he had maintained friendly relations only for business reasons.

Thomas H. Carter publicly denied that he had made a deal with the Daly interests in order to win the election. On March 4, 1889, he was sworn in and took his seat in Congress. The Butte *Intermountain* newspaper on April 14 reported that the Secretary of the Interior, John W. Noble, had requested the Attorney General to suspend all actions against the Montana Improvement Company. On September 12, 1889, the Helena (Montana)

Journal reprinted the official notice that all the pending indictments had been dropped.

To protect himself for the future, Daly then formed a lumber department as part of the Anaconda Company. He proceeded legally to purchase timberlands sufficient for all his needs.

Clark was not the kind to swear revenge—at least not in public. But after Election Day, November 10, 1888, he and Daly were basically enemies.

8

Fire!

Early on the morning of November 23, 1889, a miner named Neil McCaig stepped onto the cage of the *St. Lawrence* mine. He signaled to be lowered. Cold air whistled around his ears as he dropped down the timbered shaft to the five-hundred-foot level. As he stepped out onto the station, he found it deserted. He was early.

The night-shift men were trudging down Anaconda Road. The day-shift men were swallowing the last of their "stirabout" (oatmeal) and tea. Shortly they would swell the parade uphill to their jobs in the *Anaconda, Never Sweat* and *St. Lawrence.*

The *Anaconda* dominated the summit of the south slope. The *"Sweat"* (as it was popularly called) was slightly downhill to the west, and the *St. Lawrence* to the east. The *Anaconda* and *St. Lawrence* adjoined underground in a confusing maze of levels and crosscuts. The strong draft that was sucked down the *St. Lawrence* shaft swept through its openings into the *Anaconda.*

Lighting a candle, McCaig entered the dark mouth of a crosscut. A hundred feet farther he paused, and sniffed nervously. It seemed to him that he smelled smoke.

He hastened farther along the crosscut, his heartbeat quickening. Nothing terrified a miner more than the threat of fire or gas explosion underground. But perhaps it was only some oil-soaked rags smoldering because a careless man, going off shift, had dropped a lighted match on them.

McCaig forged ahead. The blackness turned gradually to a dull reddish glow. Then he heard crackling noises. Aghast, he saw that flames were eating up the wall timbers ahead. Even the overhead caps were ablaze! He cried out in horror.

Instead of rushing off to safety, McCaig tore off his shirt. Fortunately for him, most of the smoke was being drawn off in the direction of the *Ana-*

conda. He beat the flames with his shirt, but they worsened. Smoke swirled about his head. He was choking from the sulphurous gas formed by the heated rocks.

He stumbled back to the station. Several miners were just stepping off the cage. "Fire in the crosscut!" he gasped.

They dropped their lunch pails and grabbed a huge roll of canvas hose. Hauling it down the crosscut, they connected it to a water standpipe.

After dampening rags to tie over their faces, they trailed McCaig to the fire.

"She's spreading fast!" he shouted, opening the nozzle of the hose. When the stream of cold water hit the heated rocks, steam acrid with sulphuric fumes sizzled furiously. Sparks scattered and set fire to timbers farther along the crosscut. The miners slapped at these in vain. The strong draft fed the flames and sped more smoke into the *Anaconda.*

McCaig and his helpers soon realized that the fire was beyond them. They knew, too, that with every passing moment cage-loads of miners were dropping underground. They retreated to the *St. Lawrence* shaft, signaled and surfaced.

"Hold back! Fire below!" McCaig hollered at those preparing to enter the cage.

The alarm spread. Bells on every level jangled harshly. The hoisting engineer whipped the cage up and down until every man was above ground. When all were accounted for, John Kane, the foreman, asked for volunteers. "We've got to build a brattice [timber barricade] across the crosscut opening in order to cut off that draft!"

Many volunteered, and Kane ordered timbers lowered.

When the first smoke swirled through the deep

workings of the adjoining *Anaconda,* the few score men already underground scrambled for safety. The shaft was filling rapidly with smoke. The cage brought them safely to the surface, though many were coughing badly as they called out their names to the shift boss standing by the collar.

The hoisting engineer panicked. He bore down on the mine whistle. The earsplitting sound blasted repeatedly over the hill. Miners' wives grabbed their shawls and infants. Older children raced over ash heaps, garbage piles and fences. One look at the smoke shooting skyward and the whole city knew there was trouble at the big mine.

The undertaker ordered the dead-wagon hitched. A man ground the handle of the town fire siren. Moments later four white horses were backing into their traces. Soon they shot out of the fire hall, running pell-mell for Anaconda Road. Here they met a snarl of humanity and wagons. Women were wailing, babies crying, dogs barking and horses rearing. The whistles of the *Sweat, St. Lawrence, Parrott* and *Colusa* were all blasting.

Up to this time no lives had been lost. But the wives of all the miners not yet returned home from night shift, as well as those whose husbands had left for day shift, were frantic.

Jerry Sullivan, a shift boss, stood by the *Ana-*

conda shaft. As the miners stumbled off the cage, they called out their names. These were repeated to the far reaches of the crowd. By the time most were accounted for, Superintendent Mike Carroll arrived on the run. (Marcus Daly was vacationing in New York City.) Carroll signaled for the whistle to be silenced. Seeing the crowds pouring through the gate, he shouted, "Close the gate!"

"Mister Carroll!" the last miner off the cage gasped. "There be blastin' powder just delivered last shift on the five hunnert, and not put away yet. It be right in the path of the fire!"

Carroll's face turned pale. The miners groaned. Word of the danger spread. A big blast underground would wreck the underground workings.

Jerry Sullivan leaped onto the cage. "Let's bring that powder up, boys!"

Johnny Lyons, Henry Page, Tim Kelleher and Matt Sullivan—no relation to Jerry—elbowed on without one moment's hesitation. Carroll signaled, and a nearby cluster of women screamed as the cage dropped down the shaft.

"Get word to Kane at the *Saint*. Tell him to bulkhead all openings into the *Anaconda*. Cap the shaft if they have to!" Carroll ordered, unaware that Kane had already begun fire control work.

Down below, the miners found the flames had not yet eaten their way to the station. Normally powder was stored at a safe distance from the shaft. But this new supply had not yet been put away. The five men began moving the boxes hurriedly onto the cage. Gas, smoke and hot air made the job a perilous one. Kelleher and Matt Sullivan rode up with the first load. The cage was emptied speedily and dropped for a second load. Anxiously Kelleher stood by the collar, waiting to hear the hoisting signal. None came.

"Something's wrong down there." Matt Sullivan sounded worried.

"The gas must have got 'em. I'm goin' back down," Kelleher answered.

Sullivan put a rag over his nose and stepped onto the cage.

On the five-hundred, they found their three friends had suffocated from the smoke. They also discovered two other Irishmen, Shea and Murphy. Evidently these two, stranded in the lower workings, had crawled up a laddered manway to the five-hundred. Murphy was dead; Shea was barely conscious.

Flames were in sight now down the crosscut.

Although almost blinded by smoke, their lungs seared, Kelleher and Matt Sullivan dragged Shea onto the cage. Kelleher groped for the signal line, and jerked it.

The cage shot up.

But Kelleher had fainted. His head and shoulders toppled over too far. A protruding timber snagged his body. The cage rushed on. His crushed remains dropped to the bottom of the shaft.

Carroll saw the bloodstained cage and knew what had happened. "Poor Tim!" No one could help him. But Carroll determined that he would rescue the others.

Volunteers stepped forward. He pushed them back. He was going down into the *Anaconda* alone.

On the five-hundred the smoke and heat were so intense that Carroll could not even leave the cage. The gas was fast rendering him unconscious. Somehow he got his hand on the signal line, and then collapsed. Because there was no one else on the cage, he did not suffer Kelleher's fate. Fresh air on the surface revived him quickly.

"Seal off the shaft," he gasped. "We've got to cut that draft before the fire reaches the powder."

A crew rushed heavy timbers to the collar and across the opening, and hammered them together to form a heavy cap.

W-h-o-o-o-m!

A terrible explosion below blew off the cap. It shattered the towering headframe. Sheets of flame spurted in all directions, burning scores of men. Others were injured by flying splinters.

An hour passed before the injured were removed and the mine yard cleared. Meantime the men who had been working feverishly at the *St. Lawrence* finished the underground bulkheads and capped the shaft. Although smoke and flames continued to pour from the torn *Anaconda* opening, a crew pulled down the wreckage of the headframe and sealed off the shaft.

There was nothing to do now but wait until the fire had burned itself out.

On December 6, Superintendent Carroll had men remove the cap over the *Saint.* An hour later a stray dog was tied on the cage and lowered to the five-hundred. The cage stayed down five minutes, then surfaced. The dog was dead. Thirty minutes later Carroll repeated the test with another dog. It returned alive. He waited a longer time, then accompanied a crew underground to remove the bulkheads. The fire broke out afresh.

"Seal the mine," he ordered.

In January, Carroll was forced to order both the *Anaconda* and *St. Lawrence* flooded, as the only means of putting out the fire. For four months water poured into the workings. In April the caps were removed, and pumps set to removing the water.

Not until June 12 were the bodies of Page, Dolan, Sullivan and Murphy removed. Kelleher's remains were brought up July 22.

Depending on the deceased man's type of work and length of service with the company, the family received a lump sum varying from one hundred to no more than four thousand dollars. The union contributed ninety dollars toward funeral expenses.

Meanwhile mine-camp life, above and below ground, resumed its pace . . . until the next disaster.

9

Burying the Hatchet

The bad effects of the disastrous fire were short-lived. Soon the industrial smoke and steam from over one hundred tall stacks on the hill told of constantly mounting production and prosperity. In 1890, Butte's mines produced 25,705 ounces of gold, 7½ million ounces of silver and over 112 million pounds of copper. More than five thousand miners were employed, and the *Anaconda* was showing richer and richer ore.

Six smelters now crowded the tiny valley floor east and south of the great hill. Clark controlled two—the Colorado and Montana, and the Butte Reduction Works. Others were the Parrott, the Boston and Montana, the Butte & Boston, and the Bell smelters. Hundreds of independent mines, too small to support individual reduction and smelting works, patronized the six concerns.

Prior to 1885 the rugged mountain slopes, foothills and valley surrounding Butte had abounded in shrubs, grass and wild flowers. Gradually, as the smelters were built between 1880 and 1885, the vegetation withered from the poisonous sulphur fumes which now colored the air and made breathing unpleasant. The ores were roasted in the open air, in heaps a block long, twenty feet wide and six feet deep. No stacks were used to draw off the smoke and discharge it high in the air where it would be carried away by the wind.

Particularly during the long winter months, the smoke gathered in an immense yellow-brown pall over hill and valley. It was necessary to keep household lamps burning, even during the daylight hours. Housewives complained of the yellow specks that covered their washings. And small children were constantly getting lost in the fog.

"But why are ye cussin' the smoke?" many Irishmen argued with their wives. " 'Tis keepin' our lungs free of the con [consumption]. It do kill bugs and germs. Do ye ever hear of snakes around Butte?

"If the heaps wasn't smokin', Butte would be havin' hard times. Have ye thought o' that, woman? I'll take the smoke, and a full dinner pail, thank ye."

On frosty mornings the hill Cornishmen looked down on a weird sight: the gray smoke of thousands of shanty pipes and mine stacks and the red burning heaps of the smelters with their yellow-brown smoke rolling skyward. "Richest 'ill on h'earth?" they quipped, "Argh! More like the perch of the divvil!"

Midwinter of 1891 the Butte *Miner* editorialized, "The people are beginning to rebel." A few weeks later the city council passed an ordinance which prohibited further open-heap roasting. Henceforth the ore must be placed in stalls for roasting, and the smoke and fumes were to be drawn off through stacks "not less than seventy-five feet high."

All the smelter companies except one complied. When the Boston and Montana Company ignored the order, Mayor Henry Mueller hired a hundred men to bury their heaps under two feet of earth.

The air cleared so much that townspeople on Main Street—for the first time in years—could see the *Anaconda's* famed seven stacks, and behind them the abrupt Continental Divide of the Rocky Mountains.

Snow piled high in February 1892. It mantled the ugly gray and yellow waste dumps, the black smelter slag piles, the green-tinged mill tailings and the dirty streets. Children greeted the clean snow with a whoop and holler. On sleds, barrel staves and homemade skis, they glided down the fifty-foot waste-ore dumps. From Walkerville's icy paths they swerved onto steep Main Street. Gathering speed, they streaked past ore wagons, startled the buggy horses, and rocketed down the two-mile pitch that ended at the cemetery on the flat.

After the snow melted and the mud dried, the youngsters hammered together wagons of all kinds and continued their wild dashes down the hill. The long walk back was turned into a profitable enterprise. The boys and girls loaded their wagons with scrap wood for kitchen stoves and picked up coal along the railroad tracks. They rustled tin cans and sold them at the copper precipitating tanks. They gathered sawdust in sacks at the carpenter shops and sold this to the many saloons. They searched for empty bottles to be returned to the brewery.

When school was dismissed early in June, the boys discarded their shoes. In gangs they descended

on the livery stables and pestered the grooms into shearing off detested curls and lanky hair.

Running as free as wild colts, they streaked for Bell Creek three miles out on the flat. The stream ran clear and cold, undefiled by mine water. Screeching and holding their noses, the boys jumped into their favorite holes. The alder bushes beside the creek bloomed with shirts and pants.

Bell Creek had many bends. Each one was

claimed by a different gang. No day passed without water fights, mud fights, and even fist fights, to protect these precious water rights.

About sunset the boys retrieved their clothes, daubed mud on their bruises, rounded up the family cows pastured along the creek, and trudged home. Some made their trips to the creek profitable by supplying uptown restaurants with mushrooms and frog legs.

Boys from twelve to fifteen were expected to work during the summer. They found jobs in livery stables and grocery stores. They worked as errand boys, sold newspapers, and carried baggage at the train stations.

Evenings the entire camp braced itself for gang warfare. The gangs raided one another's hill territory and fought with fists, stones, manure and cordwood. They ripped up fences, turned over outhouses, plundered the icehouses and the grocery wagons. They filched dynamite and blasting caps for Fourth of July noisemakers, and made life almost intolerable for the cats. Whenever hundreds of buggies were parked around a tent show, it was considered great fun to unhitch the horses and frighten them into a stampede.

Butte's boys were rough and wild. Yet few, if any, questioned the discipline of home chores and church attendance. And they bought their own clothes and treats. At sixteen most of them struck off from the crowded shanties and earned their own living. They found themselves jobs in the mines and mills and regularly gave a portion of their pay checks to help feed and clothe numerous younger brothers and sisters. In time, even the wild ones settled down, married, and raised families.

Butte was ugly . . . ugly in appearance, and ugly in its sharp contrasts. Mine workings and waste dumps dominated the hill. Though many miners built small, neat frame houses, the slovenly shanties and littered streets were a blight everywhere.

Butte's wealthy mine owners, prospering lawyers and merchants formed a tight clique. More mansions cropped up on the west slope. Though pinchpenny in business dealings, Will Clark was openhanded with home and family. Kate Clark's jewels and furs were the talk of the town. When she began ordering her gowns from Paris, other women followed suit. Home furnishings, china, silver, carpeting, stables, carriages and horses—all were the best money could buy. Wealthy easterners were astonished at the lavish parties given in their honor when they visited Butte.

Marcus Daly built his mansion in Anaconda. On the west end of the town he added a grandstand, stables and racing track. Let Will Clark put on airs and buy paintings by Rembrandt, Rubens and those impressionistic French artists. Daly had an Irish passion for horses, and he was determined to have one of the great racing strings in America.

Because he was proud of the town he had brought into being, Daly started a newspaper, the

Anaconda *Standard*. Of course, it had to be the biggest and best in the northwest. Few newspapers in the nation contained more features: a woman's page, serial fiction, feature articles, political and financial colums and—most important to Daly and his workers—an outstanding sports page.

The crowning feature of Anaconda was its four-story brick hotel. It opened in 1889 with a gigantic champagne party to which notables from Montana, Minneapolis, San Francisco and New York were invited. The guests exclaimed over the marble-manteled fireplaces in each room, the steam heat, electric lights and speaking tubes, the elegant parlors. The massive back bar was a replica of the famous one in the Knickerbocker Hotel in New York City.

If the guests exclaimed over the food and wines imported for the banquet, they still were not too dazzled to observe a local miracle: Marcus Daly and Will Clark sipping champagne together. Had Clark buried the hatchet?

Only Will Clark himself could have answered that question truthfully, and no one dared ask such an impertinent question of the stiff-backed little man. But it was safe to assume that Clark was hiding his feelings for future profit.

10

The Capital Fight

One defeat had not quashed Clark's political ambitions.

On February 22, 1889, President Grover Cleveland signed an Omnibus Statehood Bill which started the process of changing Montana from a territory to a new state. Clark managed to secure for himself the presidency of the Montana Constitutional Convention. He had no opposition from the Daly-ites. An excellent presiding officer, Clark is credited with drafting the state constitution. On

November 8, Montana became the forty-first state admitted to the Union.

Governor Joseph K. Toole summoned the legislature to convene November 22. At this time the legislature, and not the people, elected the Montana representatives to Congress. This state governing body was equally divided between Democrats and Republicans. Both parties proposed candidates.

The Republicans chose two party faithfuls, Wilbur F. Sanders and T. C. Power.

The Democrats elected William Andrews Clark and Martin Maginnis. Again Daly offered no objection. Since he was now in the clear on the timber indictments, he did not mind supporting a fellow Democrat.

Friends close to both copper kings were positive the breach between them had healed.

Unfortunately neither party would support the other's candidates. Each claimed its slate was the officially elected one. Finally all four men entrained for Washington, D. C., and presented their credentials to Congress. That Republican-dominated body chose to seat Sanders and Power.

Once more Clark was thwarted, but this time he could not blame Daly.

Meanwhile Clark had acquired a controlling interest in the *United Verde Copper Mine* in Arizona, one of the world's half-dozen best. There his miners opened stopes of phenomenal width and richness. The *Engineering and Mining Journal* reported that Clark's dividends were approaching four million dollars annually. He was referred to as "the most extensive individual copper mine owner and operator in the United States."

In addition, Clark had coal and zinc mines in Montana, silver mines in Utah, a bronze factory in New York, coffee and sugar ranches in Mexico, a powder and explosives plant in Pennsylvania. He controlled numerous banks, waterworks, newspapers, street-car systems and electric-lighting companies.

About this time Montana became embroiled in a bitter squabble over choosing a state capital. Bannack had been the first territorial capital. Then Bannack became a ghost camp, and was superseded by Virginia City. Later Helena (Hél-e-na) became the seat of government, and in 1891 the legislators decided that Helena should remain the temporary capital until the people voted on the question.

Butte, Bozeman, Deer Lodge, Great Falls and Boulder immediately declared themselves in the running. Helena, as the second largest and richest city in Montana, seemed sure to win, until Marcus Daly entered Anaconda in the race.

Daly had decided that it wasn't enough to control a big corporation and be a power in the state Democratic party. The timber indictments had given him a scare. Only by turning a state-wide election at the last moment had he saved his neck. It was obvious he must control Montana lock, stock and barrel if he wished to protect himself and his company. He must see to it that nothing went on in the state without the approval or disapproval of Marcus Daly and the Anaconda Company.

Anaconda was Daly's town. He gave it life. His people ran it. No wonder he wanted it to be the state capital! He instructed the editor of the Anaconda *Standard* to launch an extensive campaign.

Will Clark actually favored Butte for the state capital. But his hide was still smarting from the defeat he had suffered from the Daly-controlled votes cast in Butte for Thomas H. Carter. Butte had snubbed him, he felt. Butte had also made a hero of Daly, and Daly had betrayed Clark. Clark saw a way to get even with both.

Clark put all his vast influence behind Helena.

First there was a primary election. Of 51,500 registered voters, almost 46,000 voted. Montana was interested in this contest. Helena and Anaconda each drew over 10,000 votes. The other towns trailed.

Montana braced for the final race: Helena versus Anaconda. But few voters were so naïve as to think the rivalry actually was between the two towns. Most of them realized it was a fight for power between Clark and Daly.

With funds supplied largely by Clark, Helena supporters bought advertising space in Montana newspapers. They wore big badges lettered "Vote for Helena," and distributed hundreds more throughout the state.

Daly countered by importing the finest cigars. Each bore a gold band stating "Anaconda for Capital." Daly had a hunch men would swap a tin badge for a good cigar. He was right.

Helenans then started a whispering campaign. They claimed the cigars were made by scab labor. Butte miners and Anaconda smeltermen threw the cigars in the gutter. They wouldn't smoke a cigar made by scab, or nonunion, labor.

The Anaconda *Standard* published information to prove the rumor was "false and despicable." Next the Butte *Miner* editorialized about "a giant corporation" trying to inflict its will on the noble citizens of Montana.

HELENA DOMINATED BY HOGOCRACY! answered the Anaconda *Standard* in retaliation. The newly rich citizens of Helena were ridiculed for their posturing, crude manners and social-climbing.

Ridicule mounted on ridicule. Libel laws were disregarded. The name-calling worsened.

The most important considerations were overlooked. Helena's rich gold placers in Last Chance Gulch had produced millions since 1864. The attractive city was centrally located, and it was the hub of great merchandising, banking, ranching and transportation activities.

Anaconda was small and inconsequential, a one-industry town despite Daly's generosity. It was located at the dead end of a small branch railroad which Daly had built only to transport ore from Butte to his smelter.

Although the entire state would vote on the choice, the deciding votes would be cast in the more populated centers of Butte and Helena. Clark and Daly concentrated on these two towns. They paid for free shows, parades, liquor and cigars. They promised new buildings and other improvements. They paid thousands to top-flight cartoonists and feature writers to lampoon each other's town.

There is sworn testimony to the fact that, between them, Clark and Daly spent $1,250,000 to

influence votes.

Helena won the election.

On November 7, 1894, the Butte *Miner* said, "Three cheers . . . This election in Montana is not only the Waterloo of the most tyrannical corporation that ever attempted to crush out the independence of the people, but it is the declaration of independence of one of the grandest people this world has ever seen. . . ."

When victory was assured, Clark and his friends boarded a special train. As Helena's benefactor, Clark meant to reap the reward. The Butte *Miner* reported that, on his arrival in Helena, "Mr. Clark stepped to the platform. He was taken upon the shoulders of several strong men and carried through a mass of cheering people to the carriage in waiting for him. . . . The carriage proceeded in triumph through the streets of Helena to the hotel with the bands of music playing and men and women cheering. . . ."

An estimated crowd of twelve thousand jubilant citizens squeezed into a public auditorium to hear Clark crow publicly over thwarting his rival.

Victory was sweet indeed, and a long time coming.

11

The Bold Buccaneer

By 1889, Butte was the largest mining camp on earth and the richest.

That summer Frederick Augustus Heinze arrived. He was twenty, almost six feet tall, with light wavy hair and an athlete's body. He wore a comfortable black suit, silk bow tie and soft felt hat. One of the new generation of professionally trained mining engineers, Heinze had studied at the Columbia School of Mines.

His first job, at a salary of one hundred dollars a month, was as a surveyor underground for the

Boston and Montana Consolidated Copper and Silver Mining Company. Heinze lived in a Meaderville area boarding house. Evenings he frequented the taverns, played the piano for fun, and made friends with the miners. Like Daly, he did so purposely to glean valuable information.

Heinze's employers were pleased with his accurate, well-drawn surveys. Had they known he made copies of these confidential records for himself, they would have fired him for such unethical conduct.

Before long Heinze was bitten with mining fever. He too wanted to be rich—and right away. He and a man named Burton leased a small claim at the foot of the east slope. His employers did not object, because this did not interfere with his surveying. Such small lease operations were common.

With the tools and blasting powder purchased at Billy Jack's Hardware Store on North Main, Heinze and Burton uncovered a small vein. They hand-sorted the rock onto two separate dumps: a waste dump and an ore dump. After showing Billy Jack samples of their ore, Heinze was allowed to charge several hundred dollars' worth of additional supplies.

When the bill was long overdue, the merchant served attachment papers on the partners. That is, he used his legal right to claim the ore on the dump, remove it to a smelter, and use the resulting profit to pay off the unpaid bill. Before leaving the mine, he told Heinze that he would have a wagon there in an hour to move the ore.

Heinze was furious. He would get even with Billy Jack! With the help of Burton he started shoveling at top speed. They switched the rock on the waste and the ore dumps.

By the time the merchant's two men arrived with their wagon, the dump bearing the attachment notice contained only waste.

After the wagon trundled off with its worthless load, Heinze and Burton rushed their ore to a different mill. Several days later they pocketed a nice profit. Billy Jack lost money because he had to pay several hundred dollars in smelter charges for having the waste processed.

Heinze had a fine time in the taverns, telling how he had outwitted Jack. Eventually he paid the bill, but not until he felt like it.

By this time Heinze was tired of mining. He didn't like calloused hands. Working his claim had taught him the high cost of development work.

Since he couldn't hope to get rich quick by mining, Heinze turned his attention to something else. Having learned that Butte smelters earned enormous profits, he made an intensive study of local operations. No wonder the smelters made money! They charged fourteen dollars for each ton of ore processed. Had they charged only seven dollars, they still could have realized a fat profit.

Heinze quit his job and returned to New York. There he tried to raise money enough to build a smelter, but failed. Once more his bright dreams of quick, easy wealth were shattered.

For the next year Heinze worked in New York City as an editorial writer on the *Engineering and Mining Journal.* In this position he had access to valuable statistics and confidential information. Secretly he piled up reports on every copper-producing and copper-marketing company in the United States. He learned that Leonard and Adolph Lewisohn had made millions selling refined copper for industrial uses. These were the same Lewisohns who controlled the mining company for which Heinze had worked—the Boston and Montana.

Then luck came to Heinze. He inherited fifty thousand dollars. Most young men would have been content to invest this and live conservatively. Not Heinze. He wanted the millions that a mining camp could produce. Instead of returning to Butte, he went to Germany. He completed additional courses on mining and metallurgy at a German university, and studied still more at Columbia. Not until then did he feel ready to tackle Butte.

Although he intended to build a smelter, Heinze felt it wise to acquire a mine first. After making inquiries, he leased the *Estrella* from James Murray. "I will give you half the profit made from all first-class ore running over fifteen percent copper," Heinze offered, "but nothing from second-class ore."

Murray accepted the offer because so far the *Estrella* had produced only first-class ore.

Next Heinze chose a crew. Officially he paid the going wage: three dollars and fifty cents a shift for miners. Secretly he offered a bonus if they would do as he told them and ask no questions.

Heinze gave his crew instructions to cave down waste along with the high-grade in the vein. They were to mix in enough waste so that the high-grade would be lessened in value. Thus only second-class ore was hoisted, and Heinze didn't have to pay anything to Murray. He could keep all the profits for himself.

Months later Murray became suspicious. He bribed one of the miners to tell how Heinze had bilked him. When Murray demanded a fair share of the profits, Heinze laughed. Murray sued in court and forced Heinze to pay him several thousand dollars. This was only a pittance compared to what he should have been paid. Heinze had opened a new rich vein in the *Estrella.* But there was no way Murray could prove this. Heinze had had had his miners fill the stopes with waste and blast down the adjacent rock to hide all evidence of mining.

With the ill-gotten profits from the *Estrella* added to his inheritance, Heinze organized the Montana Ore Purchasing Company. He started building a smelter at the foot of the east slope. In order to make an extra profit, he planned to market his own copper.

Next Heinze purchased a supposedly worthless mine, the *Glengarry.* The *Glengarry* lay south of the *Estrella,* and Heinze had surveyed the *Estrella* thoroughly. He was positive the rich vein there continued on through the *Glengarry.*

He was right. Scientific knowledge enabled him to open a very rich, twenty-foot-wide vein in the *Glengarry.*

By this time his smelter was ready for business. After proving that seven dollars a ton for smelting charges would net him a fat profit, Heinze cornered much of the business of several hundred small mine owners. His lower price also enabled other mine owners to develop idle prospects. Thus he brought added employment and prosperity to the camp. Soon his smelter was operating twenty-four hours a day, separating the copper ore from the waste. Three hundred and fifty men were employed. Six large stacks carried the smoke away from town.

Thanks to the *Glengarry* and the smelter, Heinze was gaining wealth at a fast rate. But he wasn't satisfied.

He learned that a smelter was needed at Trail, British Columbia, to treat the Rossland district ores. Leaving his foreman, C. H. Batterman, in charge of his Butte affairs, Heinze went to Trail and built a smelter there. Then he added a narrow-gauge railroad to transport ore from the Rossland mines to his smelter. This was something the Canadian Pacific Railroad had refused to do, claiming the branch line would not be profitable.

Heinze, however had no intention of staying in Canada. He only wanted to make a lot of money and get out. To accomplish this, he bought a newspaper at Trail and immediately began lambasting the Canadian Pacific Railroad. He accused it of charging exorbitant freight rates and of trying to prevent the development of the Rossland district. He made the Canadian Pacific so unpopular that the officials of the company paid Heinze one million dollars for his smelter, railroad and newspaper, just to get rid of him. Now Heinze knew the value of being a nuisance.

Returning to Butte, Heinze rented a large apartment, furnished it with a lavish hand, bought expensive clothes, and managed to get into the city's exclusive society clique. The women adored him because he was handsome and talented. The young ladies cooed over the rich, eligible bachelor.

Heinze was riding high until his foreman, Batterman, resigned and took a job with the Boston and Montana Company. Worse, he took all of Heinze's maps with him. Heinze demanded that they be returned. His request was ignored.

Heinze had to have those maps. His future operations depended on them. He spread the story of Batterman's wrongdoing. He said the Boston and Montana Company refused to return his maps. But he said nothing about the fact that most of the maps rightly belonged to the company. Nor did he tell by what questionable means they had come into his possession.

Miners, merchants and sneltermen grumbled about the shabby way a big company was treating a nice young man who had done wonders for Butte. Feelings against the Boston and Montana Company mounted. After he had the general public on his side, Heinze sued for the immediate return of all his maps. The district judge did not dare delay the hearing. Heinze won the suit, and all the maps were returned speedily.

Heinze worked feverishly with the maps. He tramped miles over the southeast and east slope. He convinced himself that the vein of the *Michael Davitt,* a Boston and Montana mine, *apexed* or outcropped on the surface within the boundary lines of the *Rarus* mine, which the company did not own. The *Rarus* was located at the top of the east slope. About two hundred feet below it lay the *Davitt.*

Heinze did some fast thinking. In his brilliant but twisted way, he saw how he could make trouble for the Boston and Montana. More important, he saw how he could turn the apex law to his advantage.

The apex law had been in effect as a federal mining regulation since 1866. It guaranteed the owner of an outcropping or apex the right to follow that vein underground, *even after it entered the boundary lines of other claims located beside it.*

Heinze sought the owner of the *Rarus,* and offered to lease it. He said nothing of his discovery.

The owner told him truthfully, "There's nothin' but second-class in her."

Heinze said he was willing to invest some money

in an effort to locate a new body of ore.

"All right," the owner agreed. "It's *your* money you're gambling, not mine."

Heinze worked the *Rarus* for months, without profit. He deepened the shaft. He ran new levels and crosscuts through tons of waste rock. Then, just as he had figured, his miners blasted into a rich vein.

Clang, clang . . . clang . . . The *Rarus* ore was rushed to the smelter. Here was new wealth for Heinze!

His miners advanced the drift along the vein; others started raising stopes to clean it out. Every day Heinze went underground to map their progress. Because of his training, he knew when the work reached the vertical limits of the *Rarus* boundaries. He should have stopped, because there was doubt that this new vein apexed in the *Rarus.* He did not call in experts to decide. Instead, Heinze hired more men so that work could continue twenty-four hours a day. They bored on into the *Davitt.* The vein richened. Heinze put more men to work, and deliberately avoided informing the *Davitt's* owners.

The sound of the blasting eventually carried into the *Davitt* levels. The foreman told officials of the Boston and Montana that he was sure Heinze was pirating ore, though he couldn't prove it. There was a thick wall of rock between the *Davitt* workings and Heinze's men.

The company hired spies to slip underground in the *Rarus* and obtain proof. They succeeded. Then the Boston and Montana Company demanded an explanation from Heinze.

Heinze pretended to be shocked. To think they would insinuate that he was hoisting ore not rightly his! He got out his maps and showed how the *Davitt* apexed on his *Rarus.* He was well within his legal rights, he said. He was only removing ore guaranteed him by the apex law.

The President of the Boston and Montana Company was a high-handed, wealthy Bostonian named A. S. Bigelow. According to an article published later in a nation-wide magazine, Bigelow rejected Heinze's explanation. He threatened to sue Heinze for the value of the ore already removed from the *Davitt.* Also, he said he would prevent Heinze from mining further in the *Rarus* until surveys and court hearings ruled on the *Davitt* apex. He denied that the *Davitt* vein apexed on the *Rarus.*

Heinze still maintained he was doing nothing wrong. He even offered to buy the *Davitt* for two hundred and fifty thousand dollars. After all, he said, the Boston and Montana people had paid only twenty-five thousand for it, and had done little to develop it. He, Heinze, and not they, had found the rich vein.

Bigelow reportedly flew into a rage. How dare Heinze make such an insulting offer! The *Davitt* was worth twenty million! He threatened to tie up all of Heinze's Montana property in court suits and prevent him from operating.

Heinze reminded Bigelow that the Boston and Montana Company had much valuable property in Butte. If Bigelow shut him down, Heinze would file countersuits and hamstring the operations of the Boston and Montana Company.

Blackmail! Bigelow charged. He promised to file suits against Heinze quickly.

Heinze should have been scared. He was one lone, young, moderately rich man against a corporation backed by the millions of the Lewisohn brothers and their wealthy Boston associates. Such a suit could be disastrous.

But Heinze was not scared. He said that if Bigelow wanted to fight, he would fight back.

Oh, yes, how he would fight back!

12

A Winning Combination

While Heinze was warming up to an all-out fight with the Boston and Montana Company, Clark and Daly continued to oppose each other. In 1896 Clark, whose private fortune was approaching the twenty-million mark, tried to elect Silver Bow County legislators friendly to him. But votes controlled by Daly defeated every Clark candidate. Then Clark tried to influence members of the entire state legislature to name him as United States Senator. Once again Daly, who had a firm state-wide grip on the Democratic party, saw to it that the representatives voted according to his bidding and thwarted Clark's ambition to go to Congress.

But politics was never more than a mere diversion for Daly. Most of his energies he concentrated on developing the Anaconda Company.

In 1895 Daly reorganized his company. George Hearst had died, and the Rothschild family had bought his share. In addition, Lloyd Tevis was ailing and wanted to get out of the company. So a newly organized Anaconda Copper Mining Company came into being with James Ben Ali Haggin as president. Fifty-four-year-old Marcus Daly was named the superintendent. In a statement published in the *Engineering and Mining Journal* and in the *Wall Street Journal,* Daly said, ". . . today, in its remodeled, reconstructed, and completed state, the Anaconda Copper Mining Company stands without a peer among the copper producers of the world.

"It can be truthfully said that in all the history of copper mining, no enterprise on so large a scale was ever before projected; no equipment for the mining, moving, treating and marketing of copper ores and their products was ever before so thorough . . ."

From 1884, when the *Anaconda* smelter opened,

until 1895 the Anaconda Company sold over 707 million pounds of copper, over 18 million ounces of silver and 83,349 ounces of gold.

And this was only the beginning. Daly had not yet begun to develop the lead, zinc and manganese properties in Butte. Nor had the *Anaconda* itself revealed its unsuspected, untold wealth of even richer, peacock-colored *bornite,* or purple copper ore.

Still very conscious of his lack of education, Daly surrounded himself with highly trained geologists, metallurgists, engineers, accountants and lawyers. But he continued to make the decisions about deepening shafts, lighting the mines with electricity, improving their ventilation, and extending the timbering without which there could not be mining two thousand feet and more underground. When metallurgists advised that the smelter be enlarged and its processing methods brought up to date, he gave the order to go ahead with the project.

Many of Daly's dreams had come true. Twenty years after his arrival in Butte, he was a multimillionaire and a colossus of mining. Gradually the *Anaconda* was reaching out and enfolding more mines. Even his race horses were winners. His favorite, *Tammany,* defeated the great *Lamplighter. Montana, Hamburg, Ogden* and *Hanover* repeatedly carried his copper-and-green silks across the finish line.

The miners in Butte didn't care two figs when Clark announced he had purchased a Rembrandt or a Corot, but they cheered and wagered heavily on Daly's racers. They also roared with laughter the day *Montana* won the Suburban Handicap. Daly had wagered one thousand dollars on *Montana* to win at odds of forty to one. He left the ticket receipt for this bet in his coat in the *Anaconda* change house when he was summoned underground. Before he returned, the change house burned down, and with it went the ticket which would have netted Daly forty thousand dollars in winnings.

Although both Clark and Daly knew Heinze, neither paid him much attention. To them he was a brash interloper of little importance.

Meantime Heinze was plotting his campaign strategy for the fight he had promised A. C. Bigelow, president of the Boston and Montana Company. Where would he start, he wondered. What had he in his favor?

First, he was very popular among the miners and smeltermen. He had spent many hours and hundreds of dollars courting their friendship. Second, he was a hero to the small-mine operators because he had cut their smelting costs in half. Third, businessmen liked him for the added prosperity he had brought to the camp.

Now, Heinze decided, it was time for all those who had benefited from his projects to do something for him.

Heinze's mine holdings were a dab compared to those of the Boston and Montana Company. His personal fortune looked mighty puny against the combined millions of the Lewisohn brothers. But a big opponent did not frighten Heinze.

Instead he thought hard and long, seeking out the point where he was weakest, most vulnerable to the enemy.

Of course! The district court. Or, to be more exact, the district judge who would hear the arguments on the *Rarus-Davitt* case and render the verdict.

Heinze could not afford to lose this suit. Therefore, he decided, he must control the judge. Luckily a local election was at hand, and Heinze had no difficulty finding the kind of candidate he needed. William Clancy was just the man. A coarse, slovenly moose of a lawyer with a long, tobacco-stained beard, Clancy could generally be found in one of the local saloons.

But Heinze was too clever to reveal his plans.

Instead he had a trusted hireling approach Clancy and persuade him to become a candidate for the office. Heinze next told his foremen and shift bosses how important it was that Clancy be elected if they wanted to keep on working. They passed the word along.

With the support of the working men, Clancy gained the district judgeship. And none too soon. In a few weeks, the Boston and Montana suit against F. Augustus Heinze was scheduled to begin.

Actually, the only positive way in which the correctness of the arguments of both parties could be proved was by means of extensive underground excavations. Neither the Boston and Montana Company nor Heinze could afford this extremely costly and time-consuming method. Thus both employed experts to reconstruct, from the maps and surveys available, charts and models of the disputed ore bodies.

The structure of the ore bodies was unbelievably complex. The experts could guess at a great many more facts than they could prove. Although they studied similar data, many interpreted their findings differently. Frequently they disagreed completely.

When the famous, historic trial began in March 1898, the Boston and Montana Company first

called its experts to testify. While these educated men stated their case, Judge Clancy put his feet up on his desk. He gazed out the window and spat frequently into a cuspidor. When he tired of one witness, he would state gruffly, "I've heard enough of you. Next witness!"

The company attorneys were astonished. Such an unheard-of irregularity! Such conduct unbecoming a judge! They protested, but Clancy overruled their objections. After a lengthy, exasperating hearing, the Judge ruled that the *Davitt* vein apexed in Heinze's *Rarus.*

The trial cost each party over one hundred thousand dollars in fees for witnesses, experts and lawyers.

The almost apoplectic Boston and Montana people announced they would appeal to the Montana Supreme Court to reverse the decision.

Heinze did not care. Clancy's verdict had given him temporary right to the ore in the *Davitt.* In the long, long weeks that passed before the Supreme Court studied the case, Heinze worked fast. He put one hundred more miners to work in the *Davitt.* His luck was phenomenal. In pushing discovery work in the *Rarus-Davitt,* he ran into one of the richest veins of copper ever discovered in the hill. Designated the *Enargite* vein, it ran forty percent copper.

Heinze reportedly took three hundred thousand dollars' worth of ore from one stope alone. Ore from this rich vein was hoisted through the *Rarus* and rushed to the smelter. Then the miners gutted the *Enargite* by filling the stopes with waste and setting off dynamite charges to cover up what they had done.

But Heinze still was not satisfied. While he continued to raid the *Davitt,* he plotted a new move. If the apex law and Clancy had enriched him once, perhaps the winning combination would work again. He planned a new attack on the Boston and Montana Company.

13

The Copper Trust

Heinze focused next on the *Minnie Healey,* located below the *Rarus* and beyond the *Davitt.* Surveys suggested that the apex of two more Boston and Montana properties, the *Piccolo* and *Gambetta,* lay inside the *Healey* boundaries.

Circulating about town, Heinze posed discreet questions. He learned that Miles Finlen controlled the lease. He had gotten it from Marcus Daly, who had bought the *Healey* years before and thought it of little worth. Hearing that Finlen had dropped fifty-four thousand into the *Healey* without finding any first-class ore, Heinze figured that maybe Finlen would be glad to get rid of the mine. Fifty-four thousand was a lot to pay for a mediocre property, but Heinze could see where the mine's nuisance value was tremendous.

Miles Finlen was only too happy to be rid of his costly dud. Witnesses claimed later that he not only bragged but even bought champagne to celebrate unloading the mine on Heinze. He had not signed the papers yet, he said, because it would take a lawyer several days to prepare them. But he had given Heinze his word that he would turn over the property to him immediately. "My word is as good as my bond," Finlen asserted repeatedly.

Since a verbal agreement constituted a valid contract in those days, Heinze moved into the *Healey*. A few days later Finlen said he had been called east unexpectedly. The papers still weren't ready, but Finlen assured Heinze that he would sign them as soon as he returned.

In the following weeks the *Healey* miners blasted into a huge, rich vein. Delighted by this unexpected good fortune, Heinze rushed the ore through his smelter. The *Healey* began making so much money for him that he put aside his plans to use it as the core of another troublesome lawsuit against the Boston and Montana Company.

Daly was in New York at the time. When Finlen told his long-time friend about leasing the *Healey* to Heinze, Daly almost exploded. Though he had not worked the *Healey* himself, he was well acquainted with the property. He had known for a long time that the *Piccolo* and *Gambetta* veins apexed in the *Healey*. But he had said nothing, purposely, because for many months Daly had been negotiating very secretly to buy all the Boston and Montana properties. This was part of his long-range program to have the Anaconda Company ultimately control the entire hill.

"Get Heinze out of the *Minnie Healey!*" Daly roared.

Finlen tried hard. First he told Heinze that he had decided not to surrender the lease.

"You gave your word," Heinze reminded him. "You said your word was your bond."

Next Finlen offered to let Heinze keep the ore he had already hoisted. Heinze still wouldn't agree.

Then Finlen said Heinze had misunderstood. He had not turned the property over to him. He had merely given Heinze temporary right to survey it.

Heinze remained suave, and immovable. There were millions to be earned from the *Healey,* and he was not giving it up.

The next day when Heinze was preparing to go

underground, a man rushed into his office. He reported that Finlen was on his way to the *Healey* with an armed guard, and planned to take the mine by force.

Heinze decided to give Finlen a surprise reception. Calling his *Healey* crew to the surface, he armed the men with picks.

Presently a wagon loaded with armed men

pulled up. The men jumped to the ground, closed ranks, and marched through the gate. Heinze and his crew swarmed toward them. Heinze was not afraid of a physical fight. Finlen might stand on the sideline and order his men to fight, but Heinze waded in with both fists to protect his property. Finlen's men fired a few shots, but hurt no one. The badly mauled Finlen guards soon retreated, and they didn't come back for a second try.

The story spread rapidly. Heinze was a hero!

Finlen now had only one resource left. He filed suit to stop Heinze from working the *Healey* until a court hearing could decide on the rightful ownership. Heinze promptly filed a countersuit and went right on hoisting ore twenty-four hours a day. Chances were that a year, or more, would pass before the hearing began. And when it concluded, Heinze knew Judge Clancy would give him the mine.

But Heinze resented deeply the way Finlen had treated him. And he resented even more Marcus Daly's trying to pry him loose from the *Healey.* In fact he began to think it was time to show the all-powerful Mister Daly that F. Augustus Heinze could make a great deal of trouble for the Anaconda Company.

Recalling a story he had overheard in a tavern, Heinze paid a visit to the courthouse. There he spent hours studying a map that showed the location and boundaries of all the hundreds of mining claims on the hill. Just about every foot of ground was taken up.

Just about . . . but not quite!

Heinze spotted a small triangular piece that lay east of the *St. Lawrence*. It was unrecorded. Thinking that there must be some mistake, Heinze set out to examine the unclaimed ground. He hunted for the location notice, but found none.

The ground *was* unclaimed.

He raced back for his surveying instruments and resurveyed the ground once, then again. Right smack in the middle of it was an outcropping—an extension or continuation of the same outcropping on which the *St. Lawrence, Anaconda* and *Never Sweat* mines were located.

It was unthinkable that so great a mining expert as Marcus Daly had let this tiny fraction of ground go unrecorded.

Within hours Heinze recorded the claim in the courthouse. It gave him indisputable right to a piece of ground seventy-five feet long, ten feet wide at one end and tapering to a point at the other. He named it the *Copper Trust.*

Well aware of the nuisance value of what he was about to do, Heinze had his legal staff prepare injunction papers. Heinze himself filed these with Judge Clancy.

When the news spread through the camp, Butte rocked to its deepest sumps.

Heinze had the audacity to claim that the *Anaconda, St. Lawrence* and *Never Sweat* mines apexed on his *Copper Trust!* Through the injunction, he sought to restrain Marcus Daly and the Anaconda Company from hoisting any further ore in these mines. And this paralyzing blow would remain in effect until after the usual lengthy court hearing, when Judge Clancy rendered his verdict.

14

Upsetting Heinze's Ore Wagon

Judge Clancy granted Heinze the injunction at 10:00 A.M., December 20, 1898. When Daly heard about it at the *Anaconda,* he was furious. It was high time, he said, that somebody upset Heinze's ore wagon.

Smiling grimly, Daly gave the order—"Shut down the mines!"

More than fifteen hundred men were already underground in the *Anaconda, St. Lawrence* and *Never Sweat.* What was this, they demanded? No work, and Christmas only five days off? Had Old Man

Daly lost his mind? Even before they shot to the surface, their anger was mounting. The *Anaconda* workers milled in the yard.

Bareheaded, coatless, Daly confronted them. He branded Heinze's injunction as deliberate, malicious and selfish. Why, the Hickey brothers had filed the *Anaconda, St. Lawrence* and *Never Sweat* claims in 1876 when Heinze was only seven years old. They had established primary rights to the veins. Daly's rights to them were also long-established. Heinze didn't have a leg to stand on!

So Heinze was their friend, was he? What kind of friend would throw five thousand miners out of work, and right at Christmas time, just to vent his spite on a mining company that had promoted jobs and good wages long before this young whip-persnapper's mother had cut his baby curls!

The miners looked at one another. The Old Man had done a lot for them. But so had Heinze. Well, *somebody* had to be to blame for this!

Someone whispered a name. Others repeated it with a growl in the numbing sub-zero cold. Clancy! What did that old reprobate care if miners' families had a cheerless holiday?

A miner shouted, "If Clancy tears up that there paper, can we go back to work?"

Daly promised that the shiv-wheels would resume turning the moment Clancy revoked the injunction.

The grumbling spread. "This layoff is Clancy's fault."

"Yeah! He oughta be hung!"

The idea mushroomed. "Hang Clancy!" the crowd shouted, and several miners ran to a shed. They emerged with a long rope.

The mob surged toward the gate.

Daly stepped back into his office. "Warn Clancy," he ordered two assistants, and then proceeded to give them some additional instructions.

Daly's men found Clancy in the courtroom. Breathlessly they told him of the lynching threat.

Dashing to the window, Clancy saw the crowd advancing. He cried out that he had been wheedled into granting the injunction. He didn't know it meant a shutdown.

The messengers pointed out that the only way Clancy could save his neck was to revoke the injunction.

Clancy groaned. It would take hours for the Anaconda Company lawyers to prepare the necessary forms. Meantime the crowd was coming closer.

If the papers were prepared, the messengers asked, would he sign them?

The frightened judge nodded vigorously.

Was there same place he could hide, they asked, until the papers were ready?

Clancy thought frantically, then named a place.

The messengers whisked Clancy to his sanctuary. Just before midnight they brought him the papers, and he signed them. Shortly afterward Daly ordered all Anaconda Company operations resumed.

Daly, indeed, had upset Heinze's "ore wagon."

Heinze decided that perhaps he had better not make trouble for Daly—at least for the present. But he kept the *Copper Trust* as a threat—or, to be more precise, as insurance.

In a few months Heinze decided he would file his second suit against the Boston and Montana Company. He would claim that the ore in their *Piccolo* and *Gambetta* apexed in his *Minnie Healey*. The *Copper Trust* would insure that Daly did not side in with Boston and Montana.

Meantime Daly announced that he was going east on a vacation. This was camouflage. First, Daly was ailing. He wanted expert care for an illness that present-day doctors would diagnose as diabetes. Second, Daly expected to close the deal to absorb all the Boston and Montana Company properties.

The doctors gave Daly enough relief to enable him to concentrate on business.

Some partners in the Boston and Montana Company were also involved in the Butte & Boston Consolidated Mining Company. One of these was Henry H. Rogers, president of the Standard Oil Company. Rogers was hungry for both money and power. He had helped John D. Rockefeller build Standard Oil into a virtual monopoly of the oil producing, refining and marketing business in America. Now Rogers proposed a monopoly of copper. He and Thomas W. Lawson and J. Pierpont Morgan would buy everything the Anaconda

Company owned, plus the holdings of the Boston and Montana Company, the Butte & Boston Company, and a half-dozen smaller concerns. They offered James Haggin fifteen million dollars for his share in the Anaconda Company, and Daly was to receive seventeen million. They would form a new company, the Amalgamated Copper Company. Rogers would be president, Daly the vice president, and William G. Rockefeller secretary-treasurer.

Always a practical man, Daly saw merit in the giant merger. Sooner or later the Butte hill would have to come under one ownership. Under the proposed merger, the *Anaconda* would still be the big mine, the core of all operations, the heart of the corporation. Daly liked that. Years earlier he had envisioned the *Anaconda* gathering within its folds all of Butte's mines. A fantastic dream . . . then.

In addition, Butte's mines were probing deeper and deeper. The Anaconda was down two thousand feet. All told, there were hundreds of miles of underground workings. Although the riches seemed inexhaustible, the deeper the mines, the higher went the cost of development work.

More important, it was becoming increasingly difficult to prove indisputable ownership to a vein or block of ore because of the tremendous breaks in the continuity of bodies of rock and veins of ore. These faultings, which had occurred in eons past, had created so complex a condition that a man like Heinze could use the law to his advantage, rightly or wrongly. As far as Daly was concerned there was no doubt about the fellow's being a pirate, even though Heinze claimed loudly that he never hoisted a ton not rightly his.

It was frightening for Daly to think of the trouble that Heinze, or others like him, could make in the future.

Yes, the Butte hill simply *had* to come under single ownership.

The negotiations were carried on with great secrecy over a period of months. On April 27, 1899, Marcus Daly announced that he had sold out. So had Boston and Montana, Butte & Boston, Parrott Silver & Copper, Trenton Mining, Washoe Copper, Big Blackfoot Lumber, Diamond Coal & Coke and the Mounted Trading Company. Also included was a controlling interest in the rich *Greene Cananea* copper mine in Mexico.

Now all of these were merged in one gigantic corporation, the Amalgamated Copper Company.

The giant would take over all the activities of all its separate parts, *including any pending lawsuits,* such as Heinze versus Boston and Montana, and

Heinze versus Finlen.

Heinze was no longer threatening a second-rate organization. He was butting his head against the largest copper concern in the world.

15

Clark's Disgrace

Heinze should have been terrified. As usual, he was not.

Through his newly acquired newspaper, the *Reveille,* Heinze smeared the Amalgamated Copper Company. He identified it with the "terrible" Standard Oil "octopus." In rabble-rousing terms he prophesied that the monopoly would reduce miners' wages and grind Butte under its heel. He vowed to champion the miners' cause. He, Heinze, would bring the mighty Amalgamated to its knees!

Overnight Heinze became the idol of Butte. He

was applauded everywhere. Miners and smeltermen promised to back him to the limit in whatever he did.

Heinze wanted not only their support but also their votes. Clancy was coming up for reëlection. Clancy had to win if Heinze was to continue attacking Amalgamated *for his own purposes.* Though he might proclaim himself champion of the workingmen, Heinze's strategy was geared to making himself a tremendous fortune, one way or another. The miners were pawns in his plan, and so was Clancy.

William Andrews Clark, always quick to use people, saw how he could benefit from Heinze's popularity. First, he ordered a secret inquiry into Heinze's financial affairs. As he suspected, despite the tremendous riches uncovered in his mines, Heinze was short on cash. A big payroll, extravagant living and development costs swallowed money faster than Heinze could make it.

Clark made a deal. He would pay the campaign expenditures for placards, badges, free cigars, free liquor, rallies and bands. In return, would Heinze stump for the pro-Clark candidates running for the state legislature? By getting his own candidates into the state legislature, Clark hoped at last to be able to get himself appointed as United States Senator from Montana.

Heinze agreed. He had no interest in the senatorship. All he wanted was Clancy's reëlection.

Clark admitted later that he spent one hundred and thirty-nine thousand dollars on that county election, alone.

The miners swept Clancy back into office for Heinze's sake. But too many who had been Daly employees before Heinze became prominent disliked the snobbish little Clark. Though they lapped up his free cigars and liquor, they voted for the Daly slate.

Undismayed, Clark determined to go to work on the legislature anyhow. It convened in Helena in January 1899. Clark used a suite in the Helena Hotel as his headquarters. His oldest son, a glib playboy named Charlie, and a tough-minded lawyer, John B. Wellcome of his legal staff, were to do the actual work.

Charlie was amused at his father's grim resolve. "We'll either send the old man to the Senate, or the poorhouse," he told his friends.

The Anaconda *Standard* warned, "Clark will be elected if money can buy his election, but in no other way."

The smell of bribery permeated the Montana capitol on a scale seldom seen anywhere.

Clark was nominated for the senatorship, but

Daly still had a firm grip on the state Democratic party. He let it be known he wanted Clark defeated. The Daly-Democrats, as his supporters were called, nominated W. G. Conrad. Other hopefuls were named, but were expected to withdraw in favor of Clark or Conrad.

The voting began.

Neither Clark nor Conrad could gain the needed majority.

Then Charlie Clark and Wellcome really got down to business. Clark Senior had furnished them with confidential reports on the Montana legislators, particularly those supporting the lesser-known candidates. They knew which men were badly in debt, or needed money to improve their businesses. Secretly Charlie and Wellcome offered several of them more than one thousand dollars each to switch their votes.

Not unexpectedly Clark's total took a jump. But not enough for victory.

Next Charlie slipped State Senator Fred Whiteside four envelopes containing thirty thousand dollars. This was to buy Whiteside's vote, as well as the vote of three other legislators.

Whiteside needed the money. However, when the legislature resumed the next day, he revealed the flagrant bribery and turned the money over to the state treasurer as evidence.

People in the gallery gasped. Legislators were stunned, and then began shouting. Newspaper reporters raced to get the story on the wires.

The Anaconda *Standard* headline for January 11 read: CLARK BRIBERS CAUGHT AT IT RED HANDED.

The Butte *Miner*, Clark's newspaper, claimed it was all a Daly plot to discredit Clark.

The sordid story made national headlines, creating a dreadful scandal.

However, after the first shock, many legislators merely shrugged. No wonder! Since the election of 1888, the voters of Montana had grown used to being either courted for their votes through favors and entertainment or told how to vote to insure their jobs. They had become accustomed to using their votes, not as the special privilege of free men, but to serve either themselves or the copper kings.

"What are the prices of votes today?" men asked one another knowingly.

"The price is going up!"

Legislators greedily pocketed envelopes containing enough bribe money to pay off a mortgage, or buy a ranch. Frequently these envelopes were tossed over the transoms of hotel rooms.

Those men genuinely friendly to Daly and Clark, as well as the few honest ones, voted out of conviction, neither accepting nor expecting rewards.

Clark's supporters, under instructions from higher up, accused Fred Whiteside of having obtained his election by fraud. After a noisy hearing, the Montana Senate unseated Whiteside. A victory for Clark!

A grand jury, hastily summoned, heard evidence supporting and denying the charges that Clark had offered bribes. In spite of the thirty thousand dollars produced in the chamber, the jury refused to indict Clark, citing "lack of evidence." Victory Two for Clark!

Now the money bags really opened wide. One by one, Clark's total of votes increased.

Clark finally won the long-coveted nomination.

VICTORY! VINDICATION! crowed the Butte *Miner.* Another word could have been added: REVENGE!

Daly hit back, fast and hard. He supplied twenty-five thousand dollars to finance an investigation of Clark's "improper election" practices. The committee gathered evidence. They presented a memorial to the United States Senate, charging Clark had been elected by fraudulent means, and recommending he be denied this great office. Twenty-five respected Montana legislators, the governor, state treasurer, speaker of the house, and two congressmen supported the memorial.

Back in Montana this same committee requested the Montana Supreme Court to disbar John B. Wellcome for his part in the actual bribe-passing. Through friends close to the justices, Clark tried to bribe them to render a verdict in favor of Wellcome. This was so insulting a move that it could only fail. John B. Wellcome was disbarred.

The United States Senate could not ignore the mass of evidence placed before it. The actual investigation began January 5, 1900. Slowly, under sworn testimony, the degrading story unfolded: Clark had spent over $750,000 to wangle the senatorship, and had then had his checkbooks and vouchers destroyed in order to attempt to hide the awful truth.

The hearings continued until April. Clark realized eventually that the verdict would go against him. With astonishing gall, he plotted to circumvent even this. Knowing on approximately what date the Senate would vote to unseat him, he wrote a letter to the Governor of Montana, Robert B. Smith. In it he resigned the senatorship, to save himself the embarrassment of being repudiated by the United States Senate.

Next, through friends, he had Governor Smith

called out of the state on a contrived pretext. The Lieutenant Governor, openly a friend of Clark's, announced that he would be out of the state at the same time. Thus Montana would be governed temporarily by the President of the Montana Senate, who was opposed to Clark.

The timing was tight, but the plot carried through without a hitch.

Governor Smith left for California, thinking he had been called out of the state on legitimate business. The Lieutenant Governor entrained for nearby North Dakota to attend a convention, and the President of the Montana Senate became Acting Governor.

Clark's letter of resignation reached Helena before the United States Senate committee investigating Clark's campaign tactics made its pronouncement: "The finding of the committee is that the election to the Senate of William A. Clark, of Montana, is null and void on account of briberies, attempted briberies, and corrupt practices of his agents, and of violations of the laws of Montana defining and punishing crimes against the elective franchise."

But the Senate could not unseat Clark because he had already resigned.

Now the Senatorship was to be filled by the Governor's appointment.

The Lieutenant Governor got his orders from a Clark agent. He rushed back to Helena and resumed his duties as Acting Governor. His first move was to appoint William Andrews Clark to fill the vacancy!

Governor Smith, Marcus Daly, most of the citizens of Montana and a great part of the nation were deeply shocked by such bald audacity. The angry governor returned to Montana immediately. He rescinded the appointment made "through trickery as fundamentally corrupt as Clark's original election." To fill the vacancy, he named Martin Maginnis.

His political whiskers badly singed, his reputation badly chewed, William Andrews Clark decided to withdraw from the bribery-paved battleground—but only temporarily.

Two years passed. Clark was adding to his millions, and Heinze to his mines.

First Heinze bought the *Nipper,* long considered a poor mine. When his miners bored into a rich vein, the Amalgamated Copper Company sued, claiming it apexed in their *Little Mina.*

Heinze then bought the *Cora* and *Rock Island,*

and turned up another bonanza. Again Amalgamated sued, saying those veins apexed in their *Gray Rock.* Heinze filed the usual countersuits. The court calendar became hopelessly bogged down with these proceedings. Lawyers for both sides had to work in relays because the preparation for the court hearings was so strenuous. Heinze rejoiced. The delays were giving him plenty of time for hoisting ore.

Another election loomed. Once more Clark and Heinze joined forces, for the same reasons as before.

As vote bait, Heinze inaugurated the first eight-hour mining shift in Montana, without a reduction in wages. Miners danced in the streets to celebrate. Clark followed suit because he had to. Amalgamated stuck to the old ten-hour shift, their men working two extra hours for the same pay.

Small wonder that this time the miners gave both Heinze and Clark what they wanted. Clancy was reëlected with no trouble at all, and even the pro-Clark men won legislative seats.

In spite of the previous scandal, in spite of Clark's public shame and disgrace, the Montana legislature finally elected him to the United States Senate. After a gigantic victory celebration, William Andrews Clark packed his bags and took off for

Washington, D. C. There, it is reported, he served his full six-year term "without distinction."

Now that Clark had no further use for Butte or Heinze, he showed his contempt by selling most of his Montana properties to Amalgamated.

Only one thing dimmed Clark's victory. On November 12, 1900, before the legislature convened, Marcus Daly, the founder of *Anaconda,* died. Daly, who had been ill in New York City all during the campaign, had won the bigger victory. His *Anaconda,* the bulwark of the Amalgamated Copper Company, pulled the Clark mines inside its coils and increased its grip on the hill.

Heinze was the only big prey left.

16

War Underground

Friends close to the thirty-one-year-old Heinze now advised him to sell out to Amalgamated. He not only refused; he intensified his raids, even resorting to underground warfare.

The Montana Supreme Court decreed that the *Michael Davitt* belonged to Amalgamated, and prohibited Heinze from mining further in the property.

Heinze ignored the order. He continued gutting the mine, while armed guards prevented Amalgamated geologists from inspecting its workings.

Amalgamated then decided to force its way underground through their adjoining mine, the *Pennsylvania.* Amalgamated miners began burrowing through the rock separating the two. When the sound of their drilling carried into the *Davitt,* Heinze moved fast. He had to prevent Amalgamated from discovering that he had removed a million dollars' worth of ore. He ordered some of his toughest miners to keep the *Pennsylvania* workmen from advancing into the *Davitt,* while others caved in its stopes.

A dozen miners waited on the five-hundred-foot level for the *Penn* men to break through. The sounds from the *Penn* had ceased.

"They're settin' the charges," the *Davitt* men guessed. They drew back.

A loud blast almost shattered their eardrums. Rocks and dust hurtled along the crosscut, against the walls, and ricocheted against the heavy timbers. From the sound, the *Davitt* men knew a fairly large opening had been punched through. Quickly they ripped open sacks of slaked lime. They emptied these into the canvas pipe line that carried fresh air into the level and crosscut. Then with rags over their faces, they raced to the cage and were quickly pulled to the surface.

As the suffocating lime dust whipped through the

opening into the *Pennsylvania,* the miners began to choke. They scrambled up manways and raced for the cages. Work had to be suspended for hours until the air cleared.

Next the *Penn* miners lowered a high-pressure water hose. They hoped to hold the *Davitt* men behind its pounding stream while Amalgamated experts checked the stopes.

Cautiously they slipped up to the opening. Five men gripped the nozzle. The watery jet rammed through. They turned it on the *Davitt* men and advanced foot by foot along the crosscut.

"Look out below!" voices shouted from the black stopes overhead as loose rocks cascaded down on them. Some were injured, but the main party kept advancing behind the hose. Four slipped into a drift, followed it by candlelight in a roundabout passage, and came up behind the *Davitt* guards. A rough fight ensued, which was finally broken up by the water.

Meantime, at great peril to themselves, Amalgamated geologists were hastily viewing as many of the looted stopes as were untouched. Another crew of miners blasted a new opening into the seven-hundred-foot level, and poured into the *Davitt.*

When the water forced the *Davitt* miners from the five-hundred to the surface, they poured more

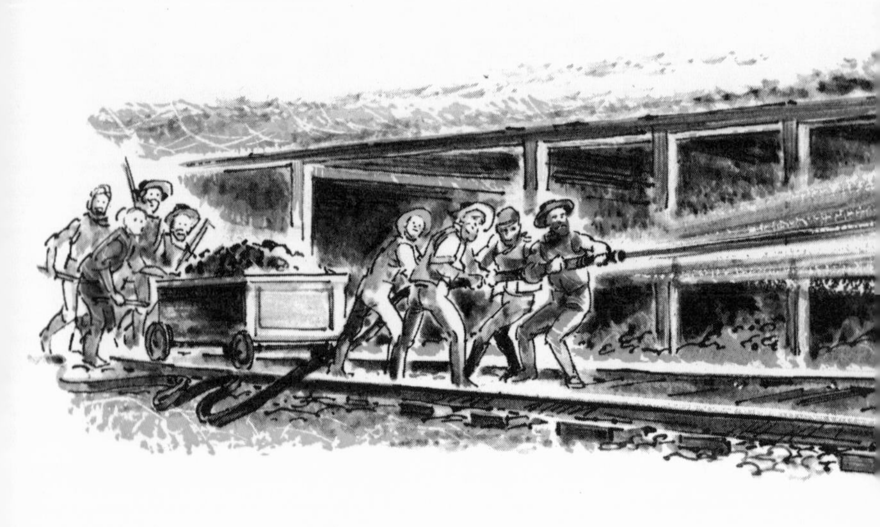

slaked lime into the ventilating pipes. The dust drove the *Penn* men back to their mine and the surface.

For several days these attacks were repeated. But all this time Heinze's miners were caving the *Davitt* stopes.

At last Heinze was ready to pull out of the *Davitt,* now reduced to a worthless wreck.

The lull in underground warfare proved to be only temporary. Heinze began to concentrate on

the *Minnie Healey.* He set his miners to cleaning out a vein that continued on into Amalgamated's *Leonard.* This was the mine named for Leonard Lewisohn, and formerly owned by the Boston and Montana Company. Judge Clancy had given Heinze the right to mine the *Healey* Heinze still used the apex law as a sufficient reason to follow a vein, even when it meant encroaching on property not his, and even when he knew the Montana Supreme Court would not accept his interpretation of the law.

When the *Healey* miners broke into the *Leonard,* they were driven back with rocks and fist-to-fist fighting.

Although Heinze was in the wrong, he told his engineers to turn into the *Leonard* the column of water they were pumping out of the *Healey.* As water began trickling through on the eight-hundred-foot level, the *Leonard* miners raced to build a dam to stop the flood. Wallace Corbett, chief engineer at the *Leonard,* sent word to Heinze. He warned him to get his miners out of the *Healey* because Corbett's men were building a dam that would turn the water back and flood the *Healey.* Heinze quickly signaled all his workmen to the surface.

Then he made his worst mistake. He told his miners that Corbett was flooding the *Healey* deliberately, thus endangering their lives.

"Drown us like rats, will he?" an angry miner exclaimed. "Let's hang Corbett!"

Shouting menacingly, they rushed for the gate. Others misunderstood their shouting, and spread the word that hundreds of miners had been drowned. Soon hysterical women and enraged men were streaming toward the *Leonard.*

When Corbett spotted the mob, he guessed what had happened. He sent a messenger to tell Heinze to call off the mob, or suffer the consequences.

Moments later, a mob of miners with ropes and picks in hand burst into Corbett's office. Facing them with a drawn rifle, Corbett demanded they stand back until Heinze arrived. He also forced them to listen to the truth: that Heinze had turned water into the *Leonard* without warning Corbett beforehand. Had the *Leonard* miners not thrown up a hasty barricade, many would have drowned. Had he, Corbett, done anything so murderous? No! Corbett had warned Heinze the moment his miners began turning the flood back into the *Healey*. How else would Heinze have known in time to signal them all to the surface?

"Liar!" some of the *Healey* miners growled as they pressed forward.

Just then Heinze arrived. Though he would not admit his part in the situation, he did assure them that no one had been drowned. And he told them to go home.

The confused miners hesitated, not knowing what to believe. Corbett had told a mighty convincing story. One that put their hero, Heinze, in a bad light. Sullen and puzzled, they withdrew.

Apparently Heinze realized the situation had gotten out of hand. He called on Corbett the next morning. The two agreed there would be no more fighting underground between Heinze and Amalgamated.

But the troublesome feud continued in the courts, with Clancy giving Heinze everything he wanted, and the Montana Supreme Court reversing Clancy's decisions in favor of Amalgamated. Finally, the big concern had had all it could take of Heinze's unscrupulous tactics.

According to the Boston (Massachusetts) *Beacon,* in October 1903, "Montana's copper kings are at war. The Amalgamated Company, in retaliation for an adverse decision by one of the state courts, has closed down its mines and mills. Twenty thousand men have been thrown out of employment."

Winter was approaching. Already snow powdered the Continental Divide. Miners' homes were cold. Soon they and their families were hungry. There was neither unemployment insurance nor welfare funds to feed them. Few had savings or money in the bank.

The shutdown continued. The Butte situation became desperate.

The miners resented the fact that Amalgamated was making their families suffer in order to get revenge on Heinze.

Miners loyal to Amalgamated spread the word that the strike was Heinze's fault. If Heinze would only negotiate fairly, the company would resume operations.

The miners demanded an explanation of Heinze. He faced ten thousand of them crowding the steps and approaches to the courthouse. In his best rabble-rousing manner, Heinze accused Amalgamated of trying to starve them into submission so they would turn against their champion, Heinze.

The miners cheered Heinze when he finished. But after they had sat a few more days in their cold shanties, they began to see Heinze's troublesome shenanigans in a new light.

Weeks passed. A delegation called on the Governor. It demanded that he call a special session of the legislature to pass laws that would settle the nasty dogfight.

Heinze fought back through his newspaper. He accused the delegation of being not representatives of the workingmen but hirelings of Amalgamated. (For once he was right.)

Governor Joseph K. Toole was in a quandary. Was it better to give in to this demand for a special session, or let the strike continue? He resented the indirect way in which Amalgamated was trying to force him to do their bidding.

Then the Governor decided to do a little horse trading with them. If he issued a call for the special session, would Amalgamated resume operations immediately?

Soon shiv-wheels were turning again, and smelter furnaces were being fired.

The special session convened in Helena. Agents for Amalgamated introduced a bill popularly called the *Fair Trial Bill.* It was just that. This bill would permit any party to any court suit the right to obtain a change of venue if it suspected or knew of prejudice of the trial judge who would hear the trial.

In other words, the Fair Trial Bill would permit Amalgamated to have its suits come before a judge other than Clancy. In view of Clancy's behavior, the request was reasonable. Nevertheless, serious-minded men in Montana and the nation deplored the obvious fact that a powerful corporation, through pressure and the starvation resulting from a shutdown, could force a duly elected state governing body to bend to its will.

The Fair Trial Bill passed without difficulty.

With Clancy no longer of any use, Heinze was ready to sell out to Amalgamated. Although his newspaper kept proclaiming him the champion of the workingmen, Heinze deserted his miners when it profited him to do so.

Seven months passed before lawyers and experts

for both parties agreed that for ten million, five hundred thousand dollars, F. Augustus Heinze was to turn over all his Montana properties to Amalgamated. He was also to dismiss lawsuits involving fifty million dollars' worth of additional property.

Still a young man of thirty-seven, Heinze moved to New York City. He meant to establish himself as a financier. Instead, he invested his money unwisely in the stock market. Within a year Heinze had lost his entire fortune!

He tried to make a fresh start with a mining property in Utah. The *Stewart* mine paid out enough to support Heinze's extravagant way of living. But the years of drinking too much finally took their toll of his magnificent strength. Heinze developed cirrhosis of the liver. In November 1914 at the age of forty-five, Heinze died at Saratoga, New York.

Not long after this the Amalgamated, after absorbing still more mines in Butte, changed its name to The Anaconda Copper Mining Company. As decades passed and the bitter story was forgotten, the company added tremendous operations in the production and refining of aluminum, zinc, manganese and lead, and allied industries. As Daly had hoped, it became the world's largest producer of nonferrous metals.

Daly's dream had come true in its fullest sense. *Anaconda* was king of the hill, and would long retain its hold on the richest hill on earth.

A LIST OF MINING TERMS WITH DEFINITIONS

assay—chemical analysis to determine ingredients and value (as-say)
blasting stick—a simple form of fuse
bonanza—a rich vein, mine or discovery of ore
bonnet—covering over cage to shield it from objects falling down shaft
bornite—horseflesh-colored copper ore
bottoms—deepest workings
bulkhead—a partition for stopping, or for protection against, fire, water or gas
cage—a frame with one or more platforms for hoisting in a vertical shaft
chalcocite—metallic lead-gray copper sulphide (kál-ko-site)
claim—a mining claim including a lode, fissure or fissure vein 1500 feet long (maximum) and 600 feet wide (maximum); a tract of land with defined surface boundaries, including all lodes and veins throughout their entire depth, the top or apex of which lies inside the vertical planes *extended downward*
collar—the surface opening of a vertical shaft
compartment—a division of the mining shaft (usually there are two or more compartments) separated by frame timbers and planking

concentrate—ore that has been crushed and the waste partially removed

crib—a structure of frames of lumber laid horizontally upon one another, usually to hold back mined ore

cribbing—close timbering, as in lining a shaft

diggings—a mining region; especially one having many exploratory excavations; also the materials dug out; singular, a shallow excavation made by a miner in search of ore; also a placer mine

ditch—an artificial water course, flume or canal to convey water for mining; a flume is made of wood; a ditch of earth

drift—a horizontal passage underground; a drift follows the vein, as distinguished from a *crosscut* which intersects it, or a *level* which may do either

dump—noun, a pile of ore or rock; verb, to unload an ore car by tilting or otherwise, without handling or shoveling out its contents

gallows frame, also *gallus frame*—a frame over the shaft, carrying the pulley for the hoisting cables

gulch—a ravine; a gully producing gold or silver

headframe—the structure erected over the shaft to carry the wheels over which the cable runs for hoisting the cage

headhouse—the building covering the headframe

high-grade—ore of great value

lead—a lode or vein of ore (*leed*)

level—a horizontal passage or drift into, or in, a mine. It is customary to work mines by levels at regular intervals in depth, numbered in their order

lode—a somewhat continuous stratified metal-bearing vein; a tabular deposit of valuable minerals between definite boundaries of associated rock

nonferrous—any metal other than iron; i.e., copper, silver, gold, etc.

ore—a natural or native mineral, usually of sufficient value as to quality and quantity that it may be mined at a profit

outcrop, outcropping—the exposure at the surface of the ground of any vein

placer—a deposit of sand, gravel, etc., containing gold or other

particles large enough to be obtained by washing; any place where deposits are washed for valuable minerals
prospect—any mine workings, the value of which has not yet been proved; an excavation showing a deposit of ore
prospect hole—any shaft, pit, drift or drill hole made for the purpose of prospecting mineral-bearing ground
shaft—an excavation made for finding or mining ore, hoisting or lowering miners and material; usually vertical, though sometimes reclining
sheave, sheave-wheel, shiv-wheel—the groove-wheel of a pulley (shiv)
shot hole—the bore hole in which the explosive is placed for blasting
single jack—a light, single-hand hammer used in drilling; drill held in one hand, while the operator hammers with the other hand
skip—a large hoisting bucket; or, an open car on four wheels, running on rails
stamp—to break up ore by machinery
stamp battery—a heavy iron pestle working mechanically in a huge iron mortar, weighing as much as 2000 pounds, and dropping 6 to 8 inches and 100 times per minute
stampeder—one who rushes into a new district when a discovery of gold, silver or other precious metals is reported
stall roasting—roasting ore in small enclosures of earth or brick
station—an enlargement of a shaft on any level, providing room for landing at each level, and room for receiving loaded mine cars to be surfaced
stope—an excavation from which ore has been extracted, above or below a level in a series of steps
stull—a timber prop supporting the roof of a mine; the top piece of a set of mine timbers
sump—excavation in bottom of shaft for collecting mine water
tailings—refuse from reduction processes other than smelting
tunnel—any level or drift in a mine open at one end
vein—any zone or belt of mineralized rock lying within boundaries clearly separate from neighboring rock
workings—all underground development

BIBLIOGRAPHY

Abbott, Newton Carl. *Montana in the Making.* 7th edition. Billings, Montana, Gazette Printing Co., 1939

Burlingame, Merrill Gildea. *Montana Frontier.* Helena, Montana, State Pub. Co., 1942

Connolly, Christopher Powell. *The Devil Learns To Vote.* New York, Covici, 1938

Fisher, Arthur. *Montana, Land of the Copper Collar.* [In Gruening, Ernest: These United States. 2nd series.] New York, Boni & Liveright, 1924

Freeman, Harry. *A Brief History of Butte, Montana.* Chicago, Henry O. Shepard Co., 1900

Glasscock, Carl Burgess. *The War of the Copper Kings.* Indianapolis, Bobbs-Merrill, 1935

Howard, Joseph Kinsey. *Montana High Wide and Handsome.* New Haven, Yale University Press, 1943

Marcosson, Isaac. *Anaconda.* New York, Dodd, Mead, 1957

Metcalfe, June M. *Copper: The Red Metal.* New York, Viking Press, 1946

Miller, Joaquin. *Illustrated History of the State of Montana.* Chicago, Lewis, 1894

Murphy, Clyde Francis. *The Glittering Hill.* New York, Dutton, 1944

Murphy, Jere. *The Comical History of Montana.* San Diego, E. L. Scofield, 1912

Raymer, Robert George. *A History of Copper Mining in Montana.* New York, Lewis, 1930

Raymer, Robert George. *Montana, The Land and the People.* New York, Lewis, 1931

Sanders, Helen Fitzgerald. *History of Montana.* Volume 1. Chicago, Lewis, 1913

Shoebotham, Hiram. *Anaconda: The Life of Marcus Daly.* New York, Stackpole, 1956

Toole, Kenneth Ross. *Montana: An Uncommon Land.* Norman, University of Oklahoma Press, 1959

Willard, Daniel Everett. *Montana, The Geological Story.* Lancaster, Penn., Science Press, 1935

Writers' Project, Montana. *Copper Camp.* New York, Hastings House, 1943

Writers' Project, Montana. *Montana: A State Guide Book.* New York, Hastings House, 1939

PERIODICALS

Anaconda *Standard*
Butte *Daily Miner*
Butte *Intermountain*
Butte *Reveille*
Engineering and Mining Journal
McClure's Magazine, May–July 1907
Western Mining World

INDEX